Rabbi Schlotz: The Transcendental Properties of Being

Rabbi Schlotz: The Transcendental Properties Of Being

By,
Michael Thomas

Shoestring Book Publishing, Maine USA

Rabbi Schlotz:
The Transcendental Properties Of Being

Published by; Shoestring Book Publishing.

Copyright 2020

By, Michael Thomas

Paperback

ISBN: 978-1-943974-34-4

Printed in the
United States of America.

No part of this book may be reproduced, stored in a Retrieval system, or transmitted in any form, electronic, mechanical; or by other means whatsoever, without written permission from the author. Except for the case of brief quotations within reviews and critical articles.

This is a work of fiction. Names, characters, businesses, places, events and incidents are either the products of the author's imagination or used in a fictitious manner. Any resemblance to actual persons, living or dead, or actual events is purely coincidental and unintentional.

Layout and design by Shoestring Book Publishing

For information address;
shoestringpublishing4u@gmail.com
www.shoesrtringbookpublishing.com

Acknowledgements:

This book is dedicated to Allan and Allison Emery who have published all twenty of my books. I can never show enough appreciation for their work. They suggest and give me ideas that showcase my books in their best light. They are honest. They have no hidden fees and what you see, with them, is what you get. I could never have found a better two publishers. I thank them with my highest gratitude.

Table of Contents

Acknowledgements: v

The Transcendental Property of Being: Day 1 1

    Let It Be Sufficient..

The Transcendental Property of Being: Day 2 2

    Requiescat In Pace or Rest In Peace ....

The Transcendental Property of Being: Day 3 3

    Buddha and Hot Water Heaters ....

The Transcendental Property of Being: Day 4 6

    In Light of Charity ....

The Transcendental Property of Being: Day 5 7

    The Stillness Within My Soul..

The Transcendental Property of Being: Day 6 8

    Until I Get It Correct...

The Transcendental Property of Being: Day 7 10

    Angels Will Then Greet Us ....

The Transcendental Property of Being: Day 8 12

    A Good Cigar - Fuck All The Rest ....

The Transcendental Property of Being: Day 9 14

    Saved In Celebration..

The Transcendental Property of Being: Day 10 16
    I Am A Dimwit...

The Transcendental Property of Being: Day 11 18
    I Say: You Too!..

The Transcendental Property of Being: Day 12 20
    A Desecrating Polemic ....

The Transcendental Property of Being: Day 13 22
    Sad Sonnet of Love ....

The Transcendental Property of Being: Day 14 23
    Peeing and The Last Judgment..

The Transcendental Property of Being: Day 15 26
    Royalties... 26

The Transcendental Property of Being: Day 16 29
    Sides of Time ....

The Transcendental Property of Being: Day 17 31
    Excerpts...

The Transcendental Property of Being: Day 18 34
    The Lady Lost..

The Transcendental Property of Being: Day 19 36
    Can You Imagine? ....

The Transcendental Property of Being: Day 20 38
    To My Liking ....

The Transcendental Property of Being: Day 21 40
    Ultimate Insecurity ....

The Transcendental Property of Being: Day 22 42
    More News To Share ....

The Transcendental Property of Being: Day 23 44
    Smoking a Cigar and Relaxed ....

The Transcendental Property of Being: Day 24 46
    Gone Forever ....

The Transcendental Property of Being: Day 25 49
    So Many Truths ....

The Transcendental Property of Being: Day 26 52
    The Rabbi Prays ....

The Transcendental Property of Being: Day 27 54
    Aroma of Life ....

The Transcendental Property of Being: Day 28 56
    As Holiness Engulfs Us ....

The Transcendental Property of Being: Day 29 58
    Floating In Forgetfulness ....

The Transcendental Property of Being: Day 30 60

   An Extraordinarily Unusual Event ....

The Transcendental Property of Being: Day 31 62

   I Reminisce How Things Change......................................

The Transcendental Property of Being: Day 32 65

   Vos Aut em Idiotae/You Are Idiots ....

The Transcendental Property of Being: Day 33 67

   We Live In Between ....

The Transcendental Property of Being: Day 34 69

   My Stature..

The Transcendental Property of Being: Day 35 72

   An Off-Tuned Radio ....

The Transcendental Property of Being: Day 36 74

   Wind-Sails Flapping ....

The Transcendental Property of Being: Day 37 76

   Pray For Me ....

The Transcendental Property of Being: Day 38 78

   Free My Eyes of Sight..

The Transcendental Property of Being: Day 39 81

   Jim's Brother...

The Transcendental Property of Being: Day 40 83

    Even A Submarine..

The Transcendental Property of Being: Day 41 85

    Thank You For Reading ....

The Transcendental Property of Being: Day 42 87

    Read No Further ....

The Transcendental Property of Being: Day 43 89

    I Will Never Appear..

The Transcendental Property of Being: Day 44 90

    Extended Time..

The Transcendental Property of Being: Day 45 91

    Culminate In Completeness ....

The Transcendental Property of Being: Day 46 92

    Frances ....

The Transcendental Property of Being: Day 47 94

    Confusion Of Books ....

The Transcendental Property of Being: Day 48 95

    Les Chants de Maldoror By Comte de Lautreamont ....

The Transcendental Property of Being: Day 49 97

    Good Night ....

The Transcendental Property of Being: Day 50 99

    Maxims ....

The Transcendental Property of Being: Day 51 101

    Blue Jays ....

The Transcendental Property of Being: Day 52 103

    Thank You For Reading My Thoughts ....

The Transcendental Property of Being: Day 53 105

    Finis ....

The Transcendental Property of Being: Day 54 106

    A Concert ....

The Transcendental Property of Being: Day 55 108

    Glad To Keep Away From Them ....

The Transcendental Property of Being: Day 56 110

    Kindness ....

The Transcendental Property of Being: Day 57 112

    So Many Souls Waiting ....

The Transcendental Property of Being: Day 58 116

    Dreams ....

The Transcendental Property of Being: Day 59 117

    Drink Deep ....

The Transcendental Property of Being: Day 60 120

    In My Care ....

The Transcendental Property of Being: Day 61 122

    Surviving Mayhem ....

The Transcendental Property of Being: Day 62 124

    Evocation Of Anger ....

The Transcendental Property of Being: Day 63 127

    My Grandmother Anna ....

The Transcendental Property of Being: Day 64 129

    Oats of Wisdom ....

The Transcendental Property of Being: Day 65 130

    Endless Majesty ....

The Transcendental Property of Being: Day 66 137

    Modern Psalm ....

The Transcendental Property of Being: Day 67 138

    I am Appreciative ....

The Transcendental Property of Being: Day 68 140

    Abnormalities ....

The Transcendental Property of Being: Day 69 142

    Jew ....

The Transcendental Property of Being: Day 70 144

    As We Breathe ....

The Transcendental Property of Being: Day 71 146

    Good luck My Friend ....

The Transcendental Property of Being: Day 72 149

    Thinking Outside A Box ....

The Transcendental Property of Being: Day 73 152

    Back Forth ....

The Transcendental Property of Being: Day 74 154

    Being Judged Unfairly ....

The Transcendental Property of Being: Day 75 156

    Inside Devotions Of Dancing ....

The Transcendental Property of Being: Day 76 158

    People Just Float ....

The Transcendental Property of Being: Day 77 161

    Faith And Hope Dead ....

The Transcendental Property of Being: Day 78 162

    Rest In Peace My Friend ....

The Transcendental Property of Being: Day 79 165

    A Detective Mundane Mystery ....

The Transcendental Property of Being: Day 80 167

    Failure Belies Best Intentions..

The Transcendental Property of Being: Day 81 169

    Ghosts ....

The Transcendental Property of Being: Day 82 171

    Rage, Rage ....

The Transcendental Property of Being: Day 83 174

    Death and Taxes ....

The Transcendental Property of Being: Day 84 176

    She Of All She's ....

The Transcendental Property of Being: Day 85 178

    It Was Apropos 178

The Transcendental Property of Being: Day 86 178

    You, Tell Me, Please ....

The Transcendental Property of Being: Day 87 182

    Mique: Hair-Dresser, Madam, Drug-Dealer, Friend........................

The Transcendental Property of Being: Day 88 184

    A Really Big Cheesy World ....

The Transcendental Property of Being: Day 89 186

    Return To Normal ....

The Transcendental Property of Being: Day 90 188
    Like a Dream ....

The Transcendental Property of Being: Day 91 190
    I Am A Writer ....

The Transcendental Property of Being: Day 92 194
    Uncle John / Aunt Irene ....

The Transcendental Property of Being: Day 93 199
    We Keep Going and Coming ....

The Transcendental Property of Being: Day 94 200
    No Echo ....

The Transcendental Property of Being: Day 95 202
    What We Cannot See ....

The Transcendental Property of Being: Day 96 205
    Unsatisfied ....

The Transcendental Property of Being: Day 97 207
    Get The Hell Out Of My Office ....

The Transcendental Property of Being: Day 98 209
    Buddha ....

The Transcendental Property of Being: Day 99 211
    Pseudonym ....

The Transcendental Property of Being: Day 100 213

    Nature's Silver Cord ....

Author's Biography 217

Also by Michael Thomas 218

The Transcendental Property of Being: Day 1

Let It Be Sufficient

I am feeling forlorn.
I cannot seem to love my sister.
She is doing her best to face life on her terms.
I think that is the most one can expect from themselves:
to accept what is part in and out of their control.
Tchaikovsky tried to commit suicide
when his life spun out of control.

It is a misleading thought that suicide will change things.
I do know that focus on positive things
will take the glamour off suicide.
Killing oneself leaves a lot left over
that needs to be made up at some point
in a ceaseless consciousness.
My best efforts are always fulfilling
when I face things squarely and work them out
to the finish.

I can fix my sister in my mind as this:
 she is human.
I am human.
Neither of us is perfect and my accomplishments
are mine and not hers.
Let it be this way.
Let it be sufficient.

Michael Thomas

The Transcendental Property of Being: Day 2

Requiescat In Pace or Rest In Peace

Hey!! I just came to a realization that the person I have the most trouble understanding and loving, will die soon. What a simple solution to all the problems this person has created. I, only hope, those problems do not follow me when I pass through the veil. Death, you wonderful cloud of cover, take away the sins of this person.

You cannot pay for a better solution, let the person pass from the earth and let the remaining children throw away all the things once loved. Watch the dumpster get filled up with boxes and pieces of a life that has ended and has no need for this junk. Let all those things, once so sacred, pile up and wash in the rains of trash dump heaven. Let the weather beat down and wear away all these things.

Most important, for me, the closets and rooms where this person slept and dreamed of those things, will be emptied and await the next person who buys this house and has no concern for the past that once occupied where they will put new things of theirs.

Requiescat in pace or rest in peace all you forces that take this soul into oblivion.

The Transcendental Property of Being: Day 3

Buddha and Hot Water Heaters

Buddha was missing things.

He did have stories of Oriental unrest that wreaked havoc on civilian women, children and men who were victims of bellicose leaders.

He did have suffering, origins of suffering, cessation of suffering and the truth of the path leading to the ending of suffering.

He did not have an answer to his own suffering as he died, like we all do, with no end to his growing old and feeling pain from his death.

We have to be careful to not idolize Buddha, like he was a Babe Ruth or Einstein of perfection. Every single person on this earth is born, declines and dies. Like the smallest element in the forest, we fade and break down into particles for the mulch of new growth.

The things that the Buddha did not have are a world war grown out of the industrial revolution that allowed Hitler and the Allies to build the greatest war machines ever developed on the earth. We still perfect creations of destruction as well

Michael Thomas

as harnessing the elements of nuclear war. We have learned to develop sun's energy for both peace and armaments.

Buddha did not have vast communication systems, nor fast moving gas driven vehicles. We would never have seen Buddha talking on a cell phone while waiting for a traffic light to turn green. He and his followers could not simply turn on their CD players and listen to the latest lute songs or how we can play and replay Bach, Brahms, Mozart, Haydn on our system hard drives.

Buddha did not hire an ad agency or an attorney to set his teachings into a book and publish it. Jesus, also, did not have our way of life.

These great religious teachers simply trudged around their travels by foot or donkeys. Buddha was born to a rich family, but they never took boat cruises or jet flights to foreign places.

We sit in our homes with stoves, refrigerators, washers and dryers. We microwave our popcorn and eat with cutlery on fine china plates. Buddha and Christ did not flush toilets or take warm showers. They wiped themselves with tree leafs and washed their clothes in streams.

I remember my grandmother who made soap out of lye and killed the chickens she cooked as if she was living in a rudimentary society. Whether we have our modern life styles, we still call ourselves followers of Mohammad, Christ and Buddha.

Mostly, we still try to love our neighbors and our gods. We still follow the scriptures laid down by past savants as rules to a good life. We still try to not kill, as we exist in our comfortable houses with furnaces and hot water heaters.

Michael Thomas

The Transcendental Property of Being: Day 4

In Light of Charity

And that from which I have seen or heard
From stories written with a sacred word
Where within or without
Sound silent or a shout
Let this stand as textual splendid
What humanity freed or was forbid
A blaze from which angels were blind
A common thread we trust and unwind
A path toward which salvation could
Offer pilgrims succor, all that is good
Let love stand alone in brilliant reason
A law unto itself; Tale with no treason
I speak to all who would deign to listen
As blatant barbarian or kind Christian
I am not a gilded parrot or eagle wing
But lowly singer of psalms I may sing
So take from me what you may
Of all I speak in simplicity say
That if you wish to enter heaven free
Then bind yourself to light of charity

The Transcendental Property of Being: Day 5

The Stillness Within My Soul

I know when the light opens windows in my eyes
Like sparks of a deity in a fire of mysticism
And the feeling in my fingers soft to velvet
Oh, you say that I am too taken with fantasies
But, all I have are the distant pieces of other worlds
Let the pull of silence keep me listening for mysteries
That help me understand why I must be born over and over
I follow no one I lead no one I am not a prophet
Nor a drunken orator
I am a bad example to lead you away from danger
I cannot react to angels until I awaken
My path is not your path
No maps
Please let me sleep till I have slipped into centuries
Forgotten sorrows dissolve when my eyes are closed
I remember the feeling of a spirit that lifts me up
I rejoice in the peace of forgiveness
For my errors are corrected
I know there is no heaven,
But the stillness within my soul

Michael Thomas

The Transcendental Property of Being: Day 6

Until I Get It Correct

The main issue is not how others benefited
or won out over me.
It is how I learned without being like those
who took advantage.
We can only grow spiritually at the expense of self-pity.
In all the dealings I have had,
I never judged or found fault with others.
I did find fault with myself
and tried my best to correct my faults.

We live in a modern age where history repeats itself in cycles. Those in power exhibit the same conditions of people who do not see themselves as others see them.

"....... forgive us our trespasses, as we forgive those who trespass against us, and lead us not into temptation, but deliver us from evil."........... What a magnificent prayer called the "Our Father"

Let us assume that we live and die
and ponder over the reasons why.

Let us assume that, by Carl Jung, July 1875 to June 1961, we have attributes that were in place before we were born and those attributes exhibit themselves as we develop.

This is so instrumental as a condition of our soul independent of our body and mind. We are eternal beings that have a stock of characteristics available for us to use as we are born, live and die.

If this precondition exists then we are left with filling in the blanks that we get reborn after death. How we come back as babies and develop, is a great mystery. One thing is certain: We do not need to remember our past lives because we have enough trouble remembering our current existence. In other words: The human mind is too limited to remember all our past lives. We do not have the mental capacity to keep other lives going in our head. We only need one life at a time. Religions have it all wrong with heavens and hell. Mark Twain joked so well when he said:

"Now then, in the earth these people cannot stand much church -- an hour and a quarter is the limit, and they draw the line at once a week. That is to say, Sunday. One day in seven; and even then they do not look forward to it with longing. And so -- consider what their heaven provides for them: "church" that lasts forever, and a Sabbath that has no end! They quickly weary of this brief hebdomadal Sabbath here, yet they long for that eternal one; they dream of it, they talk about it, they think they think they are going to enjoy it -- with all their simple hearts they think they think they are going to be happy in it!"
— Mark Twain, Letters from the Earth: Uncensored Writings

So, we are left with an afterlife of coming back to the earth over-and-over till we get it right.

I have no doubt that I am not perfect and I look forward to the succession of lives until I get it correct.

The Transcendental Property of Being: Day 7

Angels Will Then Greet Us

This thing called repetition
It saves us from perdition
We cannot escape from
Normal daily humdrum
It is ingrained within us
To expand all the fuss
Making small so large
Ships from scow barge
Leaf escaping the wind
Muck streams to ocean

I can go forever to compare
A wayward look to a stare
By now you get the drift
Lowering or getting a lift

I prefer habitual to death
What comes after breath
We live within a mystery
Where we fit on our tree
We move to a destination
Wrestle with consternation

I have married too many times
To be misled by romantic rhymes

I am a cautious careful man
More stupid than with wisdom

Socrates drank the hemlock
Caesar was knifed with shock
Death always takes its prize
From the dumb or the wise
So do not sneer at the past
Just know none of us last
And when we say: "finis"
Angels will then greet us

Michael Thomas

The Transcendental Property of Being: Day 8

A Good Cigar – Fuck All The Rest

At age eighty,
there are pleasures that remain as enjoyable forever.
Smoking a good cigar; Or good pipe tobacco.
Once a day, usually in the evening; Listening to classical music;
With my feet elevated I lean back and fall into a mesmerized
reminiscence; Sipping liquor over ice; I lose myself in thought.

This is the condition of a poet.
Sorry for expressing such predisposition,
I know that saints do not go around calling themselves saints.
They have to wait to die and some reputable person
will name them as a saint.

But, here I am calling myself as a poet.
It is not presumptuous, I am a poet of lesser circumstance.
Or, maybe great stature? I am a poet, take-it-or-leave-it.
Basic things remain true, like my aversion toward people
like my ex-wife. I was totally right in divorcing her,
and that justification stays in place without hatred or rancor.
She was impossible to live with.

Got it? She is classed with people who I have disliked like the
IRS agent who tried to take my license from me. Or the jerks
who cheated me out of large amounts of money.
Or the greedy people who took from me
without returning appreciation,.

You know, there are feelings that are constant,
like smoking a good stogie.
Nothing will diminish my understanding
of lessor people who are low on the spiritual level
and who are not worth the mention.

The lady who took her tax work from me
and paid half her bill saying that it was me
making her wait an extra time in the reception room.
What a bitch.

I can only say this: If someone removes themselves
from my association, then my life is better without them
and they are worse for it.

I cannot be a Jesus, Buddha or preacher, and love everyone.
Sometimes I do not understand: Love your neighbor
as you love yourself.
I think it should be a little more selective to say:
Love some of your neighbors who deserve your love.
Fuck all the rest.

Michael Thomas

The Transcendental Property of Being: Day 9

Saved In Celebration

Sleep is my succor
My savior redeemer
Across barriers
Forgotten areas

In dust storms of thought
Insanity is all I have got

When my soul is eviscerated
I have bled-out all my anger
Dead and desiccated
Unconscious laid-to-rest
At my worst and my best

I let the blind night
Free me of fright
Lifted alight
I am set right

Sleep is the best medicine
It is common and genuine

I know if there are gods
Their heads will wobble and nod
I will awake inside their heavens
Free of fear of being striven
And saved in celebration

Michael Thomas

The Transcendental Property of Being: Day 10

I Am A Dimwit

Nothing to say.
my thoughts are empty.

I am a rain-washed, sun-bleached empty bottle on
a scow-scattered trash heap of elevated land destined
to be a ski slope in one hundred years.

I cannot give you a glimpse of wisdom.
If you were to tie me down and beat me,
I could not confess to poetry.

I will tell you this: We all are poets. To one degree or
another, we all have sublime thoughts. Even the dumbest
looking person at the checkout lane in the super market,
has ideas equal to Shakespeare.

It only takes a few squeezes to get lemon from an orange.
Let the sun dissolve itself against a swirl of ether.
Make the moon become a book of love
for all the mementoes cast upon it by delirious lovers.

The moon is composed by layers:
Pleadings for understanding and commissions of
en-treatments from wayward souls.
I swear by the moon that I love you.
That is the best of poems:

To entreat the heavenly bodies to assist us in love.
Little moon beside the earth's orbit
To all your wishes I can but submit
Give me a piece of heaven's gambit
I am hot with passion, a fiery tidbit
I confess brilliance or am a dimwit

Michael Thomas

The Transcendental Property of Being: Day 11

I Say: You Too!

My ex-wife comes to me in the form of the devil.

She says: Kneel down and adore me. Renounce your god.

I say: Go to hell.

She says: Do you know where ice cubes come from?

I say: When hell freezes over.

She says: I had to badger you to take the garbage out and fill the empty ice cube trays in the freezer.

I say: The last person who got ice, should have filled them.

She says: Do not quibble.

I say: It has been heaven being divorced from you for over forty years,. I celebrate each year as an anniversary.

She says: You are living on frozen meals, as a bachelor.

I say: The only damn thing you cooked was "shake-n-bake pork chops or chicken"

She says: You ate them.

 I say: I could not eat them in peace because you had the house bills all laid out around the food. I could never digest my food,

She says: You needed to make more money.

I say: I was back from Vietnam and going to night school to get my degree, and you would never let me study by bothering me to take you shopping for things like new furniture that we changed in the living room three times over five years, All the old furniture assembled in the basement as a second entertainment room.

She says: Go to hell.

I say: You too!

The Transcendental Property of Being: Day 12

A Desecrating Polemic

To you dirty whore bitch mother fucking cunt.
To you bad breath dragon heart slant eyed false face female.
Your vagina is like an alley of rusty cans and jagged broken glass bottles.

When you spread your legs, moldy stench of sewer fluorescence emits its gunk onto the slimy street below your ghastly shadow.

I think of you as a brittle skeleton bleached by dead insect eaten bones.

There is nothing remarkable about your eviscerated carcass lying on the dried blood floor beneath the autopsy tray tilted into a filthy drip of your remains.

I cannot even think of you as becoming of the last layer of hell, because you are deeper than even the devil's dungeon.
I have seen the last of ripped apart lion teeth marks where you were the very bits of flesh torn away from broken skull.

I condemn you to a place greater than damnation. A place of such hopelessness that even the scraps of innocent Christians lay rejected on the dusty floor of the Coliseum after the crowds left the jackals lick their fangs for tomorrows feast.

So deserted are you in your shell of ignorance. All hope gone. All salvation rejected. All benefit of humanity left in only an ignominious lump of crud.

To say that you are degenerate does not go far enough to describe the ignominy and pervasive broken symbols of your demonic existence.

Do not even read this since your eyes have been cast out. Do not even understand since your brain has been scrapped like a limpid empty pumpkin slithering to oblivion.

You are worthless. There is not even a slight hint of grace where you dissolved like a broken rainbow of black odious lack of color.

I cannot hate any more to the limit of cursing.
I reject you forever.

Michael Thomas

The Transcendental Property of Being: Day 13

Sad Sonnet of Love

I see you a pilgrim of radiance beyond splendor.
Oh! My heart takes over my mind in a trance.
Can I but want more of you by light's endeavor,
Burning you notice for just one moment glance,

Ah! But mercy is denied as life progresses anon.
A darkness descends upon my soul engendered By
stars of night eclipsing a moon shaded in wan For
nothing. My wish is to bring you to me favored.

 So let life go on as my breath belies such futility.
There are tears where streams of beads descend.
And never is a hope for a wealth of charm gratuity.
As all seasons spill over years that have no end.

 Let all who read and understand how dust,
Turns love unrequited nay no touch-or-lust.

The Transcendental Property of Being: Day 14

Peeing and The Last Judgment

I gotta take a pee.
If you do not let me use your rest room,
I am going to piss all over this parquet floor.

I will wet right in front of the window with people passing by. An old historical photo of a summer gathering on blankets surrounding the architectural county building of Howell Michigan, shows a group of men standing on the grass laughing as they pee in front of their families.
I was so surprised at the unabashed lack of privacy.

I often relieve my bladder behind the swinging doors on dumpsters in areas where interruptions are sparse. One time, only, a cop pulled up and said with surprise: "What are you doing?" I replied that I was emptying my thermos that I pulled out from my jacket. He could not believe and he just waved his hand and exclaimed: "Empty your thermos in a bathroom."

I vividly remember the time I was leaving the hospital after my prostrate removal surgery, and I stood near my car crying because I could not hold my urine from leaking all over my pants. I have never, in my life, felt such shame. It took months of experimenting with diapers until I found the most convenient ones.

Michael Thomas

My doctor told me that the "Radical prostatectomy" procedure would result in my becoming impotent and incontinent. He was right.

We often can conjecture that Achilles bellowing over the ditch between the Greeks and the Trojans, probably had to hold his nose from the stench.

In Alaska on bivwauk at midnight, I crawled out of my sleeping bag with forty degrees below zero, and imagined a bear grabbing me as I stood shaking the drips off of my Johnson. We have customs in our society. At rest areas on highways, there are signs saying: "Dog Walk"

During intolerant racism, many cities had two restrooms, one for the white folk and one the black people.
I love how Mexican restaurant have signs on the doors saying:

"Hombre or Senorita"

Blokes or Lassies.
I think of people castaway in a small boat and wonder how long it took them to overcome the embarrassment of leaning over the gunwale or gunnel and whizzing.
This is true, years ago I was agile enough to piss into a pop bottle while I was driving.

We were chided to not eat yellow snow.

The grass cascading around my apartment complex was totally spotted from the neighbor who had two large dogs that he would release when he got home.

There was a particular person that I did not like and while no one was looking, I pissed on his car tire.

I am sorry, I have to pee and there is just no two ways about it: I have to pee. So just shut your eyes and imagine serenity in heaven where there is no hunger and no excrement. Just get on with this last judgement thing.

Michael Thomas

The Transcendental Property of Being: Day 15

Royalties

We own a small building on the back lot
near the railroad tracks.

We never use the building
and some folded empty boxes are stored in it.

We never need the boxes. They gathered dust.
The building needs a roof.

Our neighbor, who we hire for some advertising work,
wants the building.

Someone suggests that we give the building to our neighbors
with the provision that they put the roof on it and that they
figure some way to move the building to their vacant land.
It is an unspoken fact that our neighbors and some of our
employees, use the building to conduct illegal poker games
each week.

The wives of these people have been complaining about their
husbands losing money gambling.

Stories or rumors circulate that there is, also, prostitution
going on in the building that no one will admit to.

After about a month of discussion, someone rushes in to tell us that the building is on fire.

The fire damage is minimal and our owners are, kind of, fed up about the building. We have tried to find a buyer for the building, unsuccessfully.

We approached the church down the street to take the building from us as a donation,. They hemmed and hawed and finally refused to have anything to do with the building, because they said they saw the devil lurking around the building at night.

All this was going on when a train ran the tracks and crashed close to the building. Our insurance company denied any claim. The trains insurance company denied our claim. They said there was no damage and that their representatives had seen extraterrestrials fighting with angels around the building.

Someone painted on the building: "Kilroy Was Here" and "Notary Sojac". When he saw it the supervisor of quality affairs threw down his clipboard and swore at the top of his voice, surprising all of us because he usually is a quiet man; An army veteran who kept a lot of things hidden.
The restaurant nearby claimed that the face of Jesus was appearing on their toast and they blamed it on the activity going on near the building at night. Somebody wrote in that the face of Jesus looked more like the minister of the church

Michael Thomas

who had a beard and wild hair. The ministers wife denied it and stated that the face on the toast looked very similar to the face of the supervisor of quality control. There was a period when the supervisor became depressed and went into therapy.

We hired a construction company to tear the building down and throw away the scraps. Then, suddenly, the church offered to fix the roof and pay us rent for the building to store some equipment in it. We changed the locks and gave the church keys. Then photographers gave pictures to the news of séances being conducted to contact the dead within the building.

All this was going on when some local people near the railroad tracks announced that the flat roof of the building was being used to land a small helicopter owned by Tom Duke, a rich man whose house was nearby. We contacted Mr. Duke and told him to stop landing on the building. He apologized and that was that.

During all of these complicated events, our supervisor of quality control, committed suicide, shooting himself at the entrance of the building. The cops surrounded the building with yellow tape as a crime scene and the wife of the supervisor invited us to a prayer service memorial pot luck. We were so fed up by this building that we hired a writer to encapsulate the history of the building in a book or short story, and, now we receive royalties on the book.

The Transcendental Property of Being: Day 16

Sides of Time

I have built my house on a dip below Rocky Mountains.
A sliver of road sliced on the edge of a sea furious, takes you.

There are resonances of thunder
remaining from cosmic collisions.

We are never there to see or
feel the fires of creation exploding.

We are absent from the meteors dissolving around
the edges and bits of stone fusing itself against
graduations of thermal fires.

Listen to the sizzle of sea becoming glue to monster
formations.

Let this be since we can only endure
when time stretches itself thin.

I have built my house against a foolish idea of permanence.
It is only a snap of the finger and I am obliterated.

Segments of seconds skim in a stream of unintelligible
sounds. Layers of thought simply never co-lease
above the din of desolation.

Michael Thomas

You may think that Liszt sonatas
give an answer to pencil tapping.

Lose yourself into Beethoven's moonlight deliverance.
Sit easy in a chair with your feet up
as the sides of time fall upon you.

The Transcendental Property of Being: Day 17

Excerpts

So many bits and particles of words.
Norma: Hi Michael. Thanks for everything.

Unknown: Hi Michael. Great to meet you. Good luck with your publishing.

Leslie: Dear Michael. Thanks for making me laugh this morning and good call on the hippy thing.

Mike: Stop being so funny LOL

From: Dila Ljucovic and her family: Hello Michael. I am taking a moment of my very busy day just to put a couple of words together and to address some things that you deserve to know. How much we enjoy your presence each and every time you come in and visit with us. We love your sense of humor, jokes, your honesty. And how straight forward you are toward us, whether it is positive or negative. Michael you can tell how much all of us like to talk to you. You are one of a kind. You make all of us laugh out loud. Sometimes even if it is not appropriate. We are so glad we found a great friend. Over sixteen years that I have been working, I run into all kinds of people, but no one was anywhere near you, even though in the beginning you were so quiet and you were just another customer. It took you a while to come out of yourself and to find out exactly who Michael Thomas is. But now how can we put you back in the shell, ha ha ha. Michael you are a great human being with a gigantic heart and you would love to help everybody that you know in every way you can. We appreciate everything you do for us in so many ways. We all feel loved by you and we want you to know that we all love you so much too. Please continue to be our friend, now like a family member too. From all of us, here at L Georges in Canton, wishing a very happy birthday, a Merry Christmas and a healthy new year and many, many more to come. Please excuse my spelling. 12-16-2009.

Me:
Night covers over the blight of ignorance.
Dark shadows hide my wondering eyes.
My lover comes to me blind.
She lets me find parts of her.
Little by little I conjure her.

Me:
My father is the prince.
My mother is the queen.
A heritage whence
my life is in between.
Mother taught
All I acquired.
I saddled myself to her side.
I loved her till lust intervened.

Divested of passion to acquire my need.

Me:
Rabbi Schlotz and Detective Sergeant Mundane
 These pieces do not fit into any cohesive whole.
They are recorded here for reference only and always for gratitude.

The Transcendental Property of Being: Day 18

The Lady Lost

It is full and proper to deny the lady.
She assumes a pride not worthy of her personality.
Blabber fills in where intelligence is missing.

Nothing of merit collects within or without of her presence,
I asked her what her opinion is of intimacy.
She proclaims that she is waiting for a soul mate
to captivate her.

I listen and wish to not be that person.
I will do without her for now and into the future.
 "What is that bulge protruding from your belly?"
She says it is caused by her nerves.

 I rise and escort her to the door with a perfunctory goodbye.
(So glad to get rid of you. Words not spoken)
She leaves and I dispose of the insipid cookies
that she left for me.

 I wash my hands and go to sleep alone and quite secure.
 Of all the women I have known,
her rating is totally out of range.

It is proper to deny this overeager fop.
She takes my money and gifts without a thank you.
I have paid a small price to rid myself of her greed.
 Let me tell you this: She has no idea of who she is.

"Oh would the power, the gift give us. To see ourselves as others see us." - This premise is wasted upon her.
She is lost and does not know it.

Michael Thomas

The Transcendental Property of Being: Day 19

Can You Imagine?

The thing about Richard Bleznak, Sullivan & Smith and the Jewish Community Center, is that I always felt comfortable there with them.

I never told them that I was of Arabic descent. I think, that, after a while, I had lost nationalistic characteristics as an American born in Detroit. I always wondered if they thought of me as Jewish? Probably so.

These were real rich people who built in the outreaching communities of West Bloomfield Michigan and never talked about the holocaust. Remember, this was 1950, just five or six years during which Judaism was adjusting to over six million of their people being horribly tortured and murdered by one of the most infamous acts of humans possible in Germany.in World War Two.

Benjamin Kastle was one of the children of the steel company. He owned many eating establishments in the area. I was the CPA auditor of his companies. It was my job to make sure he conformed to Accounting Principles. He was a private person who had many sexual affairs that turned into employment opportunities for the ladies afterwards.

It was funny, each week phone calls would come in saying that Ben referred them and jobs were given to keep these women away from Ben's wife and family.

Ben was ostentatious and flamboyant. He gambled heavily and one time he called Robert, his head accountant, and gave him information about twenty restaurants that he had won in a poker game.

Ben did not like me because I discovered how he was in cahoots with an insurance agent, for over-billing a hundred thousand on a fire loss for which he shared fifty thousand or one half with the crooked insurance agent.

Sam, my boss, rushed over to the offices of Ben and had a long private meeting during which Sam tried to fit the theft into the audit report.

These were very rich people and they assumed an elevated position of morality as being above the law.
I was just a small time auditor struggling with a family and trying to pass the CPA exam, which is harder than the medical exam.

I remember two men: Burt Binder and Jim Lark, who developed sections of land with roads and street lighting to sell plots for houses to Sullivan & Smith. During my audit I watch these two men play act a simulated meeting where they each took the part of their adversaries bargaining positions for one of their sales. I remember these two men saying that they were so rich that they did not have to wake up each morning to go to work and it was a situation that made them uncomfortable. Can you imagine?.

The Transcendental Property of Being: Day 20

To My Liking

I have lived alone for over fifty years.
No need to accommodate or make allowances.

Waking up at two in the morning and lumbering to the living room, I sensed someone else on the couch. Of course it was just an instantaneous thought as I switched thinking to my destination, at the computer.

I have become very selfish of my personal time always being free from constrictions. It is an ingrained way of life - living alone.

There was a brief time when my son was visiting and he stayed the night.

It was well over forty years ago and I remember vividly that he was thinking of living with me. I shut the door on that situation quickly and told him to move his stuff out and make his own home somewhere else.

I knew he was disappointed but that's the breaks.
He got over it quickly and here I am solo and satisfied,.
Ladies, on rare occasions, wake and make breakfast, but they move away quickly. I treasure the freedom of solitude.

Quietness gives me the chance to think clearly. I hear strange sounds from my various neighbors and imagine the

displeasure of their kinds of music or conversations if I had to live with it.

My classical music is a sedative. My aloofness is my genuine pleasure.

I do believe in reincarnation and maybe I will have to live again with another person, but that is down the road.,
I do know that when I turned fourteen, I left home and delighted in it.

On a quick stop to my old home, my father asked me what that car was in the driveway. He said: "You are only fourteen and do not have a driver's license."

I said that was my business.
He said who was the girl in the car.
I said, that was my business.
He said, what are you doing here.
I said, I was hungry.
Being a son; Having a father and mother;
I was a very closed-in person.
Somehow the world has fitted into my personality.
That is just the way it is and it is to my liking totally.

Michael Thomas

The Transcendental Property of Being: Day 21

Ultimate Insecurity

We live on a small planet.
We live in proximity to neighbors.
We live in the fear of annihilation.
We live in the fear of death.

Life is more comfortable with
faith, hope and charity.

It is impossible to satisfy the majority
when the minority is unsatisfied.

There is only one way out of despondency –
 to love oneself and your neighbor.

"Of Faith, Hope and Charity, the importance of charity can scarcely be overstated; It has been called the greatest of all things, without which we are nothing. We should listen and seek to understand others. We should give to and seek to serve others. We should care for and love others." From Brett G. Scharff's book: The Most Important Three Things in the World (February 12, 2013).

The reason that charity is important is because it is coincident with "Love your neighbor as yourself........."   All religions profess this as the cornerstone of life.

Love is a multifaceted word. To love, one must forebear. One must make distinction between staying away from aggression and coming as close as possible to empathy,

The basis of love is a diminution of ego or self-importance.

When we lower ourselves in meaning,
we raise ourselves up in love.

There is no answer to the meanness surrounding us.
Civilization will flow with the cycles of fear and security.

The only secure meaning in life is our ultimate insecurity.

The Transcendental Property of Being: Day 22

More News To Share

Sightings of Jesus
Sandals in hand
Toga disheveled
Dust covered eyebrows
Apostle-less alone

When was the last time he had a good meal
Stepped out of a shower refreshed and toweled off

We are lucky to have ear phone buds
Listen to rock, beaten the blues

We park our car and find a family restaurant
With cabbage soup and crackers

Jesus looks through the window
We offer him a hand signal to come in
He refuses
He has no money

He is aware the cops will give him the bad eye
So, he keeps moving into the shadows
Afraid to tell people that he is the son of god
Knows he will be laughed at, so he looks away

Where will we find our savior
Living in a one bedroom loft
What will be his behavior
A graceful smile
A touch so soft

Will we hand him a dollar
Hold the door open for him
As he enters and adjusts his collar
His eyes blink to the neon dim

We have no reason to mention
That we might have hidden sin
We will chose fruit that is soften
Count our blessings and listen
Release our heart from its prison
Let salvation come streaming in
There is always a point to reason
But insanity has its own season

A sonnet or free verse
Smile or a curse
A Chinese proverb
Nobleman or serf

We are better off in silence
Speak little and act wise
Paucity or abundance
Each have their own prize
The next time we see Buddha
Remind him that Jesus was here
Tell him to come back tomorrow
We might have more news to share

Michael Thomas

The Transcendental Property of Being: Day 23

Smoking a Cigar and Relaxed

When we listen to a Chopin nocturne,
we are at the top of our game.

There is no higher music to please us.

No matter whether we are rich or poor,
we still derive the same satisfaction.

When we read Joseph Conrad describing a character or scene, we are at the ultimate level of enjoyment. No other words or author can please us as Conrad does.

Funny how the best things in life are at our disposal no matter what our place in society is.

Often I will drive down the street and feel that all the cars around me are equally safe and comfortable. It does not matter whether I have a Rolls Royce or a Ford. I am lucky fortunate to have four wheels. an engine and a steering wheel at my command.

I was married for a short time with two children. I experienced the joy of a honeymoon that did not disparage my divorce and estrangement. I never remarried, because it would have been redundant. I had no need to go through the

process twice. So, for forty nine years I have been single and very well situated. I, also, do not need the comfort of a woman constantly poking me in the ribs to see if I am awake or dead.

There was a time when I had six employees and a growing CPA firm. I went through the heights of expansion until I could no longer control what was going on. I scaled down, paid off over two hundred thousand of debt and now I am comfortable with cash and a partner who is half my age and twice smarter than me. I divested myself of three partners who took all they could and left me. I was the better for them going away.
I think the best way to describe my situation is to say that I am fortunate by modulating my life with no more excesses and no more depravity.

I have outlasted all the stereotypes and remain individualistic and true to myself. I have no idea how "There but for fortune go you and I." But, here I am smoking a cigar and relaxed.

The Transcendental Property of Being: Day 24

Gone Forever

Sometimes the imagination is too small
to encompass an event.

A small town local sheriff accompanied by a lawyer who only litigated two cases aside from his bar tending job, drove out to a cemetery with a shovel.

They were following up on a scrawled note left in a safe deposit box from a deceased loner who had no existing family. When they left, Marcie, at the hair salon, called her aunt who called a friend who called a friend from a close by town nursing home.

The two located the spot on the note and started digging where a grave was supposed to be.

In the long history of buried treasure, there abound stories of peg-legged pirates who put their sword through all in their group and hauled off chests full of gold or jewelry to their ships and sailed away.

The sheriff and lawyer sweat as they broke clods of dirt and dug deeper than they conceived was necessary. The sheriff called for help from town and three deputies arrived with their shovels.

The hole got bigger and bigger with no results. The site expanded into an accompanied grave site identified as an elderly person who had relatives in the town.

Bigger and bigger, the hole turned into swimming pool size. No caskets revealed themselves. Finally the diggers hit a resounding sound of clinking against some metal chest. The dirt slowly was removed around the item and it revealed more chests below each other. A total of six chests, too large and too heavy and needing a hoist brought out from town by a large flatbed truck.

Just as the chests were raised and placed surrounding the area, a sound was heard in the distance of two trucks roaring with dust raised from their wheels churning up the desert in clouds.

Simultaneous with the group attempting to unlock one chest, the two new arriving trucks backed up and, lowering their tail gates, two men began spraying the site with machine gun fire. Everybody hid behind their cars. Bullets pierced metal and both sides erupted in returning bullets whizzing back and forth.

It took some time with exploding gas tanks and such for all people involved on both sides to die. No one escaped. No one lived.

When the neighboring law offices cleaned up the mess, three days had passed and the only existing living relative of the final grave where the chests were buried, was contacted.

She was bed ridden in an assisted living home. Her name was Rosanne. She had been a secretary to an abortion clinic and still had ties to the manager to whom she simply signed over

all the money from all the chests. The final tally amounted to too much to even be counted.

After so many legal intricacies, the money ended up in the hands of people who believed in the right to a woman's choices.

Right to life advocates complained to no avail.
A hospital was contacted and doctors who curtailed births, were paid to curtail more and more pregnancies.

The halls of the hospital resounded with the cries of unwanted embryo's bouncing off the silence. No one paid attention to the wailing that could not be heard. All was, seemingly, at rest in peace.

These things passed beneath the dust of generations turned into hills and mountains of compressed memories: Where a group of caskets were buried in the large hole and markers announced the gone-forever people beneath.

The Transcendental Property of Being: Day 25

So Many Truths

Each step to acquire new knowledge, leads to further steps. The acquisition snowballs into an avalanche of tremendous information.

I, sometimes, become overwhelmed with data
to the point of confusion.

One thing remains core to this search and that it takes so many forms and situations that center upon time, place and circumstance.

In my youth, I have been assailed with bits and pieces of things that led me to append what I learned to so much other bits that the whole gets larger and larger.

From the time I could think straight at age ten or so, I took the bus to the main library in downtown Detroit and would spend the days selecting book after book to read till I rushed to catch the last bus taking me back home.

I have slept with books surrounding me
in every bedroom I ever occupied.

Michael Thomas

A grade school teacher quickly erased the name "Decameron" by Giovanni Boccaccio from the chalk board, saying that he apologized for telling us a book that was forbidden by the

church. It was too late. I had written the name down and found the book in the library and relished the great work written during one of the plagues when people were quarantined. It was a book describing the antics of priests and nuns having sexual intercourse. A concurrently written series was "One Thousand and One Nights" also known as the "Arabian Nights" published in 1704. This book was composed during one of the Black Plagues in Europe. It is less explicit but similar to Boccaccio's structure.

I remember the situation of the library on Gratiot Avenue in Detroit called the Mark Twain Branch that smelled of the pine tree wood used building the walls of a sweet odor that I have locked in my memory while I read and read books all day in the silence of the stacks. .

I have been nurtured inside libraries with stories of life in so many different places where knowledge is kept between covers of novels that intrigued me intently, .

I feel so sad, that now, my computers have taken the place of libraries. And I can find anything I want on Google or Amazon that has replaced the physical need of card catalogs and Dewey Decimal systems.

My school graduation year book, listed me as "Library Assistant" and chess club. While others were noted for their sports achievements.

Mrs Eleanor Ladendorf and Virginia McHarg where the two ladies in control of the high school library who taught me so much referring authors and books to me. They allowed me to

file volumes as well as keeping order in the rule of not talking in the library.

In one library I would read while the pet cats who lived in the library would curl up on the desk staring at me while I read. In the army, I always found places where books were kept and I would find respite perusing history and such in the quietness of such delight.

College libraries were another favorites of my need for education.

Recently my pursuit of things has led me to studying the I Ching as well as the many works of Napoleon Hill, who is so interesting.

One thing is for sure: I will never outgrow the quest for information added upon information that keeps my mind open to so many truths.

The Transcendental Property of Being: Day 26

The Rabbi Prays

The rabbi prays.
In the robes of spirits.
Collected of memories gathered from incidence,
in the fervor of penance.
I am what my ancestors passed to me through
the lines of mysticism.

I am confined to my humanity.

Expounded by my unlimited consciousness.
I am the rabbi, mullah, priest of adventure.
Strip away the mark of Cain for I raise up my brother
from the grave.

I transcend my parents who languish in a deserted paradise.
Heaven dissolves into a vapor of frankincense.
The idolatry of volcanoes hovers over towns asleep
with no warning of the impending avalanche.

I darken the sun and blur the stars
into their canopy of pin-points.
I allow the moon to embarrass itself
as a blush mirrored light.

I am the rabbi of deep cavities
where ghosts await their actions.
I am the principal and biblical exegesis
hidden in scrolls uncovered.
Allow me my pretentious humility.
I am both obscure and vivid in scale.
A psalm of silence falls from my lips
and all around me vibrates love.

Michael Thomas

The Transcendental Property of Being: Day 27

Aroma of Life

To the reader. Steel thyself to not turn away from words. Let thy mind clear itself to fathom all that is written here in truth. That magnanimous becomes insular. To heroes lost within pages of manuscripts long forgotten. Giants of place and circumstance waste away to dust upon an indescribable desert of naught but wind and pitiless dust.

To the fallen we ascribe only our sympathy. Their time came and went in the space of an immeasurable spot.

Where our telescopes searched blank space between timorous stars, they blend into black. Those whose vanity sat them through direction, now are cast off as lacking signs. Those whose egos exploded beyond their stature, are now without name or significance.

We measured their achievements. We cataloged their images and closed the chambers of their banishment to a desultory diminished dungeon.

Further than horizons falling off ends of a flat history, they scurry for any aid.
They cannot help us with our day-to-day struggles.

We are weary with hope. We wish for respite from adventure.
We seek rest from any consideration
and let our minds focus on inner silence.

This bitter fruit is not for the mother or her progeny. This
compost is furrowed into rows of declination.

I am not your advantage. I am not your safe haven.
I can only dream of purity,
for it is wafting past me as aroma of life.

Michael Thomas

The Transcendental Property of Being: Day 28

As Holiness Engulfs Us

If I could take you back in time
Where antediluvian creatures
Crawled beside my nose align
Prehistoric moans of beasts

Filled air with resonate fear
Upon wet scratchy clover
I would spread you thin
In a blind prostate curl

Inseminate cavities dark
Hidden wombs of desire
Birthing monster groans
Illiterate newborn worms

Squirming in innocence
Of their sucking hungers
Freeing you of insecurities

Gaining over that will - god

Heavens portals open
Entangle us with lust
Welcome strange paradises
Ever blooming languor

This is what I would speak
Silently into palpitating heart

A prayer for your redemption
Through my fingers splitting
Your raised breasts aroused
Exhaling all tremors mouth

Open to tongues lapping
A fever of blessedness
Subsides over our nakedness
As holiness engulfs us

Michael Thomas

The Transcendental Property of Being: Day 29

Floating In Forgetfulness

Listening to Bob Dylan or Beethoven Piano Trio Number two in G major, I derive the exact same measure of enjoyment.

The beauty of sound goes past my ears into a space in my secret heart where I am taken away from my surroundings and placed in a new venue.

Awareness accentuates a fresh reality that must be what a god feels doing something like creating a flower or embellishing a sunrise.

Often, viewing a sun slipping past a horizon, the moment when it disappears brings a sadness. It is a one-time sun thing, that never will be repeated exactly like the one that just passed.

The transient stretch of beauty can be formulated in first, the appearance of something going to happen. Second, the build up and exposition central to things. Third, the dissolving and fading of a vision into oblivion.

We are born. We go through our life. We wilt and die. Our experience is added to our primary soul like part of a crossword puzzle of all our lives existing in a mystical body of interrelated sections.

Creativity can be synopsis-ed as introduction, development, recapitulation/ending.

When we die, we cannot come back to our past life because it is imprinted upon our divine nature.

Bob Dylan, in an interview, said that he does not remember the songs he wrote in the past. He said he does not like singing the old songs. He is on to new things.

We are sitting in a train and when we arrive, we can only faintly remember the scenic trip that got us where we are. We can only try to describe the past in terms of what we felt while we were going through it.

I remember my marriage as a whole of meeting, joining and then ending the relationship. I do not regret, I only rehash.

For thirty years I had a friend. When she died, it was like an "anticlimactic" happening that I surmised as beautiful in its origination and sweetly reminiscent in its ending.

Pathos, is one of my favorite words because it embodies joy and opposite of joy.

Hearing Beethoven's piano, violin and cello trio 2 creates within me a pathetic feeling of relish.

I will go to sleep with the music floating me in forgetfulness.

Michael Thomas

The Transcendental Property of Being: Day 30

An Extraordinarily Unusual Event

Max and Milroy, (I found out their names later) were playing in the hall outside their room.

I sensed they were lonely and I gave both of them ten dollars each. They went down to the gift store and came back with bags of candy and junk.

They were tearing packages off of candy and eating like imps in a circus and laughing.

Their mother, Mildred, (I found out her name later) came out to the hallway and saw her children totally preoccupied. She was amazed since she expected them to be bored and irascible. I told her what I had done, giving them money, and she was just flabbergasted. She went into her room and I heard her explaining the situation to her husband, Joseph, (I found out his name later).

Joseph came out to the hallway in a bathrobe and questioned me for my motives. I assuaged him into understanding that I was not a child molester and (sort of) hinted that he was not a good parent for not taking any interest in his children. He ignored my chiding. He (sort of) half thanked me and left the kids in the hallway; Going back into his unit without further ado. I heard him talking to Mildred and both of them seemed (sort of) out of sorts.

Meanwhile Max and Milroy giggled and dribbled all over their Halloween-like-gotten gains in total oblivion. Other residents peeked out of their doors or wandered past them without a jot of interference. Their looks of indifference spoke to their non-concern.

 I am a sedate person who stays out of trouble. I left the door to my room slightly ajar to be sure that the kids were not in trouble and I went about reading my book (in half interest), while the situation wound itself out for over an hour and half. Joseph and Mildred, (I never found out their last name) had food brought up on a tray and whisked their children into their room. They cleaned up all the empty wrappers and juicy-saliva-laden, half eaten candies.

Their door closed and silence pervaded the area as I shut my door and slept.

The Transcendental Property of Being: Day 31

I Reminisce How Things Change

I never found her too alluring.

She was kind to me and allowed me to live in her basement during a time when I was homeless and recovering from being rejected.

I viewed her as extremely emotional. This is a terrible term, because we all ride our feelings to heights or lows that suit our situations. In her case, she would get sorrowful or teary over things that you or I would pass over.

She sat on a curb at midnight crying heavily. I sat beside her to comfort her. She explained to me that John was in the hospital dying. John had a long standing wife who was his support. My friend imagined a relationship with John as her college English teacher. She never had a physical sexual relationship with him, but conjured a deep connection with John that just did not exist between the two of them.

I could not believe how my friend could extend being a student to being a lover. The reality of it was too much for me to understand, but I simply held her hand and told her that it would be all right.

I never found her attractive. She was simply a nice person. I used to sleep on the bed in her basement and listen to her having sex with different people even while her children scampered about the house.

My situation was temporary. It was winter. She, her lovers and her children would leave and the front and back door was always left open causing the furnace to always be on. To me, it was negligent for them to do so, but they did not have much respect for the University housing authorities that rented the unit to her.

Years went by after which I remained in contact with her and, in time, her one unmarried daughter passed the bar exam while the other daughter became a born-again divorced evangelist with four of her children. This daughter's ex-husband lived with the daughter and drove around the country in a dilapidated car selling bibles door-to-door. Strange!.

My friend remained living in the house that her and her ex-husband had bought and never ever made any repairs. The house was exhausted. The house was a shack on the edge of a pristine forest. Whenever I went to her house, wild animals would half hide in the trees close by.

My friend was private with me. She went to Germany and had a baby with the man married to her mother. She later told me that it was her way of getting back at her mother. I was befuddled to say the least. But she went ahead and had the child who grew up to quit school and work construction while living with his mother.

My friend's son was a hunter who tracked and killed creatures in the forest near their ran-sacked house. My friend would accompany her son into the woods and also shoot anything that moved around her.

I tell you that she was emotive in an unreasonable manner. One time when we were in a restaurant eating, I handed the person at the table near us a twenty dollar bill since I saw they were having trouble paying the bill. My lady friend was disconcerted that I did so. I was silent. She berated me for doing so. I was silent. She got angrier and angrier at me not defending myself and she simply got up and took a cab home. I, courteously packed up her food and took it to her house where she accepted and ignored why she had acted so.

One of the aspects of my friend was her and her lawyer daughter visiting my house and walking around examining my furnishings while gushing with enthusiasm over each item. I felt they were just expressing their extended surprise about things that I considered mundane.

Later, toward the end of my time with this woman, they both verbally jabbed at me and deceived me into doing work for them that they did not pay me for. I brushed it off and my interaction with her diminished to very little. She just went out of my life and I felt no guilt or regret. Thirty years have passed and I reminisce how things change.

The Transcendental Property of Being: Day 32

Vos Aut em Idiotae/You Are Idiots

Nothing in my life can surpass my anger unleashed.

I was sitting with my parents and they were showing me books, medicines that they kept stashed away.

I sat patiently while they paraded bottles of pills for prescriptions that predated the founding of Rome; little pills that some doctor had written in year nineteen seventeen; pills that had lost their potency long past, decades ago.

There was a book of instructions, resembling what Alexander the Great would have referred to in destroying Tyre and Sidon when he built roads in the ocean to reach the besieged enclaves, and enslaved or killed all its citizens.

I scared my parents half to hell by throwing their sacred treasures into a waste basket and screaming at them for being so stupid.

Cesar wrote "Gallia est omnis divisa in partes tres"
I hollered that: "ignorantia fecla" or, "ignorance is divided into two parts", describing the two of them.

Michael Thomas

My hair stood on end as I ranted in a hoarse voice: "In my life, I have thrown away everything when I found a new doctor."

How could you base your life on things that mean nothing, now?

Starting all over means just that: Starting all over.

The lights blinked. Silence was deeper than empty space between planets. Mom and Dad were crying as I pointed my finger at them and shouted: "Vos aut em idiotae" or "You are idiots".

The Transcendental Property of Being: Day 33

We Live In Between

I wander and question
My thoughts can't compare
To what pilgrims petition
For Jesus to be there

Where a breeze flows-on over
Where sun meets the stars
I am drunk on green clover
There's a river gone far

A halo hovers over us in grace
We are blessed by circumstance
That no darkness can erase
A rainbow over which we glance

There is a time to our limits
A dwindling in our hearts
Morning sun born in it
All sadness departs

See my tears stain a face
A cloud in my eyes
Mourning in lace
Evening dark dies

Michael Thomas

A forest of wishes
A valley of blues
Manna delicious
Laugh in my shoes

Let's all get together
Join up for a chance
Say goodbye to winter
Spring brings us a dance

Tomorrow will fly
Past today's dream
Hear us say why
We live in between

The Transcendental Property of Being: Day 34

My Stature

I like to think of myself as special, idiosyncratic, one-of-a-kind, hero, above-the-common, spiritual, a seeker, a finder.

I picture myself as a boulder rather than a mundane shooter marble.

I am afraid, that, in a crowd I would shy away from notoriety. I would just blend in to the background. I wish I was, but I am not a Jesus.

If you came to me, as Bill Vettori did in 1962, in the army, asking me questions about god and religions, I am not the information person to give you or him answers. Bill would ask and I would repeat insignificant facts out of the Catholic Catechism or conflicting Biblical passages. And, he would tap his cigarette ash on the floor, grind it with his boot and stare with revelation as if he was saved from perdition. Truth is he is, for sure, in hell with all of us who think we are smarter than the rest.

I am a fledgling. I am a fish out of water. I am an eagle with clipped wings. I am a fox with no sense of smell. I am a coyote who has lost his night-crying scream. A lion with no claws. I am a giraffe with a short neck. I am truly a banana with no peel. An apricot with no pit.

If you came upon me on the ground in a nature hike, poked me with your staff, I would turn over like road kill and not move.

All of these things are true. I am but a piece of trash on a wind-swept hill, conglomerated with all the rest of that garbage.

Let this be said of me at my funeral: He was nothing special and his behest to world fame consists of a cough as he died. Just as I bleed out, tell the sheriff to leave my boots on because my feet will stink too much.

I am:

A corsair without a sword.
A sword without a hilt.
Yea!, I am a gun without bullets.

I remember on a cold night when mortar rounds were ripping the buildings apart in explosions, I ran and landed in a foxhole with my machine gun and Murphy, who was supposed to bring the ammunition in metal boxes, was dead and he never arrived.

A lady I once knew imagined that she was holy enough to sit close to god after death. I know my seat will be so far away I could not see god even if I had a telescope.

So, sorry for boring you about my scant significance. Do not read any of my published books because you will come away disgusted.

Reserve your comments without praise. Let me lie beneath a rock undiscovered even by rodents eating bugs.

In Debussy's nocturne of the sea, in the siren passage of that grandiose piece, I will fade away like in a storm wasted upon ocean turbulence.

The Transcendental Property of Being: Day 35

An Off-Tuned Radio

My ten speed narrow tire bike was kept inside the garage. I would ride it at night when worlds slept.

I would ride it in circles where asphalt ended in dirt gravel surrounding desolation dark areas too far away for my imagination to encompass.

I had a fear of what I did not know of my neighbors, Their house lights would twinkle between tree branches.

I wanted my father's gas station to not be deserted. My father had no idea how to make it successful. Windows were broken. Moss covered isolated pumps and cobwebs glistened in night's street lamps.

Cars would stop, then move on. My escape plan was to dash into half opened doors and hide till drivers would lose interest in such eerie-ness.

I think back on this time since house and garage were sold and torn down. Replaced by a monolithic residence that spoke of wealth.

A swimming pool ran past trees on a walkway
up to the new house.

You would not know that once I lived here
and left to find a life away.

There is a sadness to past invisibility. Our lives exist in a past
that has no semblance. Our memories hold past events
enshrined within our hearts.

My recollection of that misty garage,
my bike and my father's deep voice from windows
telling me to quit riding and come in
to go to sleep was ingrained into my ears
like an off-tuned radio.

Michael Thomas

The Transcendental Property of Being: Day 36

Wind-Sails Flapping

We arrived.

Our ship encased in freezing water threatening ice. The horizon was barely visible from horrific winds causing snow to mass in clouds like a desert storm.

Crew in good spirits, looked forward to our mission. We had been warned of other groups finding trouble on their adventures. Since we were, mostly, traders rather than settlers, our arrivals had mixed reaction from local residents. They often tried, without success, to find our caches for raiding. We were very cautious; our trips inland were always covered by our agents lagging behind to look for spies. We were instructed to not kill but just hold them to be released when we finished.

Tracking inward, we reached where directions led us from last expedition.

Cave covered, resisting our picks and hammers.

Sven, one of our best, hit surface of metal door. We cleaned all square corners but could not find control to open it. Sven fastened a stanchion to ceiling and swung high with his ax.

He hammered at the top incessantly. We reread notes from last year's crew, all to no avail.   Sven found a small

indentation that miraculously pierced our ears as door creaked open barely missing Sven's rope.

Little did we know what we would find. Our mission was to retrieve bone and cloth fragments left by our last members. Often our mission would be to categorize inventory of trading goods. This time we were to find other things from our past. There is often a feeling of sacredness as our eyes and fingers touched the past relics of our ancestors. Special linens wrapped what we needed. Tender threads tied all packages into small bundles which were placed into a wood vessel embossed with our emblems.

Sven lead a prayer and we retreated in solemnity.

The metal door reacted to our shutting it with an exhausted whoso of air.

As we sailed home, few words can describe crews elation over finishing the task and our prayers for a safe return rose above the wind-sails flapping.

Michael Thomas

The Transcendental Property of Being: Day 37

Pray For Me

I know my uncle wanted to kill me.
From the inheritance my father left me.
Uncle was always inept.
He lost all his money and dad gave him loans.

After dad died,
my uncle was at my back
waiting for advantage over me.

I do not remember why I agreed to climb onto our pointed roof and address all who were waiting for a speech and money thrown to them - part of an annual custom continued by my dad after all serfs were freed.

I have a deathly fear of high places, but there I was with my uncle behind me and me clinging to roof tiles with much fear. I yelled to my uncle that I wanted to get down, that I was in too much pain.

He laughed and told me to hang on.

I inched backward slowly and reached for his hand which he offered but kept withdrawing, until I managed to grab onto the wood reinforcement at roof point and pulled myself up gradually till I was on my knees.

Uncle blocked my way to the elevator and I shoved him with a surge and made it into the elevator. Before he could react I pushed "Down" and heard doors close with relief.

I made it to the basement and Frank, was emptying trash into bins. He helped me get to my rooms.

I do not know what to report, other than I now have hired a protection person who Frank referred me to.

If word gets around that I am dead, please investigate my uncle and pray for me.

The Transcendental Property of Being: Day 38

Free My Eyes of Sight

addle eyed
'wipe that smile from your face'
white man speak with forked tongue
'do you think that is funny? I'll show you funny:

Go to your room and I will tell you when to come out '
when I became blind, I could see
when I look into your eyes, I fall in love
Zeus gave Tiresias gifts of prophecy and longevity
Tiresias was blinded for seeing Athena bathing

Athena gave Tiresias an ability to see the future
in place of him seeing the physical world
Oedipus blinded himself when he realized he had killed
his father, Laius and slept with his mother, Jocasta.

pin tail on donkey, blindfolded
rain pelted me in my eyes temporarily blinding me
beautiful beautiful brown eyes, I'll never love blue eyes again
mine eyes have seen the glory of the coming of the lord
he is trampling out the vintage
where the grapes of wrath are stored

he had a heart of gold
and silver eyes so cold

Diogenes carries a torch
searching for an honest man

a fox can see
rabbit is blind
hawk is free
dove is kind

out of sight
out of mind

I cry
the rain comes
I smile
the sun returns
blinded by the light
revved up like a deuce
another runner in the night
in the eye of a hurricane there is silence

my number one son
fails to see what is in front of him

I left my home in Memphis
for a home in Tennessee
I'll never have women love me
in the dread land of Abilene

Michael Thomas

come out come out wherever you are
I see you up close to me and from afar
little do we know what will be revealed to us
when we close our eyes to all those we trust

Cyclops traded one eye to see a future
god gave in return the day of his death

color me a rainbow
let me see a light
my heart will glow to
free my eyes of sight

The Transcendental Property of Being: Day 39

Jim's Brother

Why do you pull over, get out and stand at that fence for five minutes and stare?

"Someday I will tell you", Bill would say to me.
Bill used to stand at another fence facing empty fields. He would inhale deeply, pound his chest and tell me how wonderful the cow manure smelled.

But I never knew what was on his mind most of the time. Jim threw his cigarillo onto cement tile and smashed it with his decorated Red Wing boots. Jim's car was a Porsche. He would brag that it could outrun the cops who were frustrated not catching him. They knew who he was. Everyone in the building and in town, knew who he was. There was quietness as he walked around standing the loose Two-By-Fours straight to match each other on the walls of the shed. Funny, cause his dad owned the lumber yard as well as other yards in the country.

Dennis, back room supply clerk, hated Jim. Most everyone hated him for being a spoiled child. His dad waited for Jim to grow up and get over being wild so his son could take over the lumber yard business. Jim did drugs and grew hallucinogenic mushrooms in his basement. Jim owned a Harley motorcycle.

Big chrome bike with cat tails streaming and straight-pipes, meaning there was no muffler. The sound was deafening.

An aspect of Jim's extravagance was his Bichon Frise Chinese rare breed dogs as well as his parrot that he had named: Harley. Jim kept the parrot in a cage next to Dennis's desk. Dennis hated to feed and take care of the parrot. Secretly he wished Jim would take care of his own parrot. Dennis taught the parrot to say: "Harley is a stock holder" which was repeated by the parrot over-and-over. Jim's wife would not let the parrot in their house.

Everyone watched as Jim stood up leaning all wood against walls in an orderly fashion. Jim was ridiculing Dennis for leaving the wood on the floor.

There was whispering. Without Jim hearing, a murmur went around: "He is jealous of his brother."

"What brother? We have never seen the other brother." Bill, one day, turned to me and said: "My other son is there." He pointed to a cemetery. "He died on a horseback ride. Thrown from the horse."

Jim left the room and I saw a ghost of his brother following him in sadness.

The Transcendental Property of Being: Day 40

Even A Submarine

I am not an adventurous person.

After Vietnam, I stayed in Detroit,
passed my Certified Public Accountant exam
and worked for over fifty years servicing clients.

I had two children and remain divorced
for over forty five years.

I am now, relatively rich and have published twenty books.
Tell me, then, why I am on a huge ocean liner and cannot get
off this megalithic boat till it arrives in South Africa in nine
months.

All I did was answer an internet add with an obscure story
about my parents anniversary and I was led to a ceremonious
gang plank to board this boat off the Detroit river.
It is so hard to believe that it took so little time for a boat to
travel St Lawrence Seaway's leading to Atlantic Ocean
vastness.

There is no one on this boat who seems to understand that I
want to get off and go back to Detroit and be left alone.
I was very tired and when I awoke It took me three hours to
try to make an international call on the phone and I gave up

Michael Thomas

when someone told me it would cost over a thousand dollars to even try to communicate with my partner.

I was desperate to eat and three people came to my sumptuous room with carts of food containing every imaginable dish of chrome plated servings.

I tried to ask for a representative or captain of the boat and it was misinterpreted that I wanted a prostitute. Two slattern women in fancy dresses were brought to my room. I immediately sent them away.

Then two more women of Asian extraction were sent to me. I cannot believe how hard it is to make direct talk to these people. I just want to be removed and go home.

I threatened to jump off of the boat and asked for life preservers. They just laughed and pointed to an ocean map trying to explain how I was some small dot in the water.

I ate and went to sleep, hoping when I awoke, some relief would come and someone would helicopter me away or summon an American Coast Guard boat, even a submarine, like in the movies.

The Transcendental Property of Being: Day 41

Thank You For Reading

It is a feeling you get when you think of something. Like the first time I heard Rachmaninoff's second piano concerto second movement, I became totally absorbed by the music and I remember being in the sun setting living room of the old house with cut glass windows standing in middle of stereo machine and I was only ten years old. I was captivated by this concerto and I have been to this day.

It is the feeling of being unhappily married and so full of despondency that I thought my insides would explode. I could not wait to leave that house and wife and two kids. I was totally correct since the marriage was incorrect and gaining neither her nor I any credit. Time has proven me correct since I never remarried and my life is balanced correctly now.

The feeling of disgust over a man I idolized who turned out to be an avaricious crook who cheated so many people. I got out of his clutches and sent him a message itemizing all the terrible things he did to people who trusted him. He never responded and I never lost any money with him, only my precious time that added to zilch with him.

I can go on and on about feeling about things. I think our feelings can rotate between negative and positive. When I passed the Certified Public Accounts exam, I felt so good and remembered sharing my elation with my co-workers.

When I was discharged from the army and flew out of Vietnam arriving home, I waited for just the right moment and went to a fishing site on the Detroit river where I could sit on weathered dock pilings and watch shadows from Canada shimmer across the iridescent water at night. It was a place of mental refreshment. I dreamed of it always. I remembered being within sight of people fishing on lawn chairs catching cat fish and throwing them back into the water. I remember always eating cone island hot dogs and drinking a coke. Beautiful emotion encapsulated forever within my heart.
It is always the feeling that arouses my creative process I feel a poem than I write it. "I feel therefore I am" could have been coined in place of "I am a thing that thinks" by Rene Descartes.

I believe that every single one of composers pieces of music came about from their feeling first.

I will tell you this, my feelings of caution saved my life during battle with bullets whizzing all around me. I knew I could not be killed as long as I stayed aware of myself enclosed within a cone of safety. I felt safe.

Sorry for making you read this long story.   Thank you.

The Transcendental Property of Being: Day 42

Read No Further

I, red devil of delirious, spell
Cover me invective
Collapse blue bridges
Where colors fuse
Into formidable

I blue angel of amorphous
Could you see through
Bring to me sheep
Counted by rows

I let you into a term
When all else fails
Close out a world

Swing upwards
Like bulimia
In curds
I bellow Achilles

Sore heeled
Paris cows
Let fires recede
Bury all not breathing

Michael Thomas

Recast this world into fantasy
I, red devil of desire
Clothe you intemperate
I wish only for finality
It is over between us
Read no further

The Transcendental Property of Being: Day 43

I Will Never Appear

We are born of sorrows.
Deceits we overcome with constraints.
We are born of wisdom.
Built into us like batteries.
We are desire.

For food, sex and love.

I sleep uneasy in remembrance of past injustice.
I wonder how much can one absorb of petty aggravations.
When I look into your eyes are there similarities of thought?
My neighbor is ungrateful.

I cannot make her be anything but what she is.
I will stay away from her because she can teach me nothing.
Even those I associate with, have a limited effect upon me.
History, art, words of great writers;
that is what moves me to change.

Leave me to my books and reading lamp.
I will not even answer the door.

Pound and stand waiting for me to never appear.

Michael Thomas

The Transcendental Property of Being: Day 44

Extended Time

It has been a while since last writing.

In between sessions, I had to solve three thorny problems successfully so.

My pride is self-contained and not shared with others, except you who read this.

Our aggravations irritate us. We lose sleep. We obsess over them. Once they go away, we are so relieved and satisfaction recedes as time passes.

Time is our gauge in life. We remember back. We think ahead. We concern ourselves over present conditions.
Let me tell you a story: I was riding a three wheel child's bicycle and my daughter was watching along with her mother. I have two children: a boy and a girl. I am estranged from the girl. My son is my friend.

I was riding this bike and I wanted my daughter to be proud of me. My ex-wife was influencing my daughter against me. I was pronouncing my innocence and seemed to be making headway in converting my daughter over to liking me.
Then, I woke up and dreams end, but reality continues in extended time.

The Transcendental Property of Being: Day 45

Culminate In Completeness

Naked baby sucks on supple fleshy nipples hanging down its mother's warm chest.

There is no more honest lovely image a world can give us. That literal juice cleavage with a tiny protuberance between clasping crevice of female hips stills vibrates from expelling a breathing creature that increases our population by one or more.

A new soul slurping for tits even as a rope tether of imbecilic cord waits to be snipped after doing its job of feeding. All so innocent, void of orgasm, but replete with a glow of serene pleasure as great as a sunrise or verdant garden greenery.

We men are but witness to events that only our counterparts can experience. We males are left out of the show stopper of maternal instincts. We are jealous viewers.

Heaven greets such spectacles with a smile. Gods are pleased. And cycles culminate in completeness.

Michael Thomas

The Transcendental Property of Being: Day 46

Frances

A boutonniere she squashed against my car door handle.
She sighed and removed her blouse top. I sighed and
pretended to ignore her breasts falling over a loose brassiere.
Frances Mary Louise DePonio wore my engagement ring.
Her two spinster aunts peeked out of a darkened window
parted curtains. Her father was a cop. I always imagined him
arresting me for kissing his daughter.

She talked as I gently touched her abstractly.

She talked about her dead mother or her brothers and sisters
that she was expected to watch over as an oldest sibling.
She talked how she hated a role as a replacement mother.
There is an emotional hurricane hidden in hearts of
inexperienced high school students who catalog sexual facts
as they learn,

God has played us so well to keep the babies coming. We are
given pleasure in exchange for pain of child rearing.
I danced with her as my palms sweated. I could not wait to
get her in my car.

After army discharge and new job, I ran into her in Ann Arbor's library parking lot. She had been divorced from her first husband. She acted ebullient to see me and brashly suggested she come over my house to visit and knit.

I instantly refused her, because no prom memories could rekindle my past with her.

She had changed and she commented that she liked the man I had become. I knew myself and did not regret getting back into my car alone and closing the door knob that her wrist flower had once touched long ago.

The Transcendental Property of Being: Day 47

Confusion Of Books

Confusion of books.
Lead, halter, drop us over ideas in rainfall of images.
One proposes war.
Another peace.
Books leave us in a quandary.

From moments after pirates walk planks,
Centuries following storms,
Millennial monster shifting of stars,
Books burn slowly as governments are rewritten.
Popes censor hearts of raw sympathies.

We are confounded by too many lives.
We are born again, new, fresh, to save us the memories.
Books revive our anticipations.
If one book can be remembered as better than another, then take both.

I read with mistrust. I read looking forward to perfection.
Books are imperfection masked as perfect.
I will tell you this: Every book I gave away to libraries or friends, created a groundswell of spirits following me forever.

The Transcendental Property of Being: Day 48

Les Chants de Maldoror
By Comte de Lautreamont

Les Chants de Maldoror: Novel by Comte de Lautréamont

A writing caught between opposites.

A writing of superb images beyond ordinary
and beautiful past normal.

One is held by words of wonderment that Comte de
Lautreamont uses in putting this book together.
No other book, that I have read, is so spellbinding and forces
me to stop and catch my breath as I put the book down and
think upon these sentences.

Raw thoughts of a devil described in simile, pointillism,
extended comparisons and first person point-of-view.
At first one is aghast at being forced to think about death and
afterlife in such dramatic fashion.

It is a rendering of evil past evil,
yet carrying us to acceptance of decency refuted.

Michael Thomas

This author died at age twenty six and this is his only book. He does not need another book, since this one encapsulates a main topic in over three hundred pages with such verve. The writing is reviewed as: Surrealistic. It goes beyond to scare and shock us with such vividness.

As I read this, I cataloged it in my memory forever.

The Transcendental Property of Being: Day 49

Good Night

Not sure what you want to hear.
That I am feeling fine?
How are you doing?
World turns histories over-and-over.
Meteors slam into us.
Plagues kill sixty percent of population.

It was easy to get a job when those two infestations ended.

Earth plates shift: Volcanoes bury lots of people.
Harvey Weinstein is getting what he deserves.
I hate daylight savings time changes. Remember:
Spring forward/Fall back. Too many clocks to change.
My ex-wife still hates me after forty five years of divorce.
My daughter hates for absolutely no reason understandable.

Both eat out of same cereal bowl.

My son is my friend. I feel so grateful for him.
My partner for over thirty years is honest and between
Her and I we have over one hundred thousand tucked away.
Took my two sisters out of will:
They take. give naught – but greed!

Michael Thomas

My partner will get all money when I die. She deserves it. I have twenty books published and I am so proud. They can be found at Amazon or Google by typing: Michael Thomas Poetry.

The global virus is changing our world.

We are so lucky to have a Hubble telescope.
I am over eighty years old. My doctor asks me why I am so healthy. I ask him if he wants me to stoop or cough or pretend. He laughs.

Tired of giving quarts of soup to my neighbor, who never says thank you.   Go figure.

I wear gloves and keep the banister leading upstairs, washed of germs.

Oh!   I have been reading "Tibetan Book Of The Dead". What a fascinating book.

I can write you a rhyme:
Morning comes again,
Like a regular event.
I live seasons absent,
Of dire love's passion.
I am tired and headed to bed.
Good night.

The Transcendental Property of Being: Day 50

Maxims

World has its own agenda.
We are pawns within life.
Do your best to be kind.

When you die, your thoughts
will determine how you are judged.
There are no mistakes that cannot be corrected.

Look upon all you do as being in constant flux.
We can go backwards or forward
while fixing things in the spacious present.

As we grow.
As we get older we age like cheese
or a rare bottle of wine.

We rid ourselves of guilt
as we rid ourselves of unbalanced thoughts.
I have always looked down upon our heroes
who commit suicide.

Suicide is not a way out,
it is a dead end,
Suicide is a circle that must be broken by succession.

Michael Thomas

We succeed by acceptance of pain and death.
Pain is its own panacea.
Pain reaches a pinnacle of relief
by our control over causes and remedies.

We are remedial by laws of nature
that give us answers when we become a pursuer of truth.
Truth is a plateau of understanding
that can have no other answers
but a finality in rationale layers that can go no further.
Truth is our lifeboat of grace. Truth is a harbor of tranquility.

Wisdom is truth.
Wise thinking is silence in a clamor of sounds.

Wisdom comes when ignorance fails.
Do not read this as a bible.
Read this as if being pointed to your own path.
The path to truth has no diversions.
There are no roadblocks
when we push on-and-on
toward an healing light that encompasses us in peace.

The Transcendental Property of Being: Day 51

Blue Jays

See saw
La la de law
There is a cat chasing a mouse
See saw

I watch and put odds on one or the other
An egret swoops over a tumbling wave like a wind surfer
Turbulent swells crash into each other
At night when all is quiet a small ripple traces a porpoise route
Jason leans over the gunwale and takes a whiz
It is so easy to be free of land as deck tips topsy-turvy
Seasick sailors retch into blue ocean over railings
Someone said: Go down below so you do not see
the horizon tipping, but it did little good
Older seasoned mates giggled at us

Life is a series of plateaus
where we rise then sink below our expectations
I came from a family of lazy thinkers
It took me very little time to tire of them
As they all have gotten older,
nothing has changed in their characteristics
Schubert died of syphilis
He tried all his life to surpass Beethoven,

Michael Thomas

but never did
I want to be like Beethoven
and see seagulls imagining their screeching

Famous people, mostly, cannot control their sexual appetites
Marlon Brando shunned fame
but could not control his eating
and became very fat toward the end of his life
Thomas Merton, author of: Seven Story Mountain,
died in 1968 in Thailand

Catholic church denied his conversion to Buddhism and buried
him in Abbey of Gethsemani Trappist Cemetery,
Nelson County, Kentucky, USA - as a Catholic
I visited his grave and all that I thought
was the birds sang for him

When I die,
I want Robins in the morning
and Blue Jays chattering away for me

The Transcendental Property of Being: Day 52

Thank You For Reading My Thoughts

Inevitability of seeds
Squeeze lemon over tuna noodle casserole
get juice on fingers

As you eat, you spit out the seeds onto a napkin
Sometimes you can take seeds out of your mouth
As tongue separates them

It is strange: This seed thing
A papaya has more seed than fruit
Peach seed clings

They are gritty as mouth rotates them clean
We are seed of our ancestors.
The apple does not fall too far from the tree

Like kind tend to gather together
I learned how families who built the great cathedrals
Of history, all kept having children who kept the vocation alive

I was born from an uneducated mother married to a butcher
I rebelled, completing college
And became a CPA who wrote books

Michael Thomas

My three siblings all became butchers
And never went to college

Diverse evolutionary paths spin one way
And another
Sometimes seeds get confused
But acorns usually become oaks

I think that seeds fulfill their destinies dependent upon
Circumstances surrounding their entry into a circle of life
Conifer seeds depend upon forest fires to germinate
I can go on and on but I will bore you
Thank you for reading my thoughts

The Transcendental Property of Being: Day 53

Finis

We found him hung but we have questions
He was a murderer who committed suicide
Why did he kill himself? Maybe guilt?

Murderers might meet justice
On another side of the veil of life and death

Our concern is to investigate circumstances on this side of life
We have a suspicion that relatives of his murdered victim
May have staged this killer's suicide

We found particles of acetylcholine
Within the blood of this suicide
How could he have committed suicide
If he was immobilized or paralyzed?

All family members could have been located near suicide
Our superiors are asking that we spend no more time
Or money on this case since it is clear
That the suicide was murderer
And some insidious form of balancing
Has taken place by his death.

Finis

Michael Thomas

The Transcendental Property of Being: Day 54

A Concert

Phones chimed. Cars arrived / departed exhaustively. Conductor Samovitch followed his retinue into Mrs. Grants mansion like the arrival of a potentate.

He was lodged with favor during this weekend stint of much anticipation.

His program with Detroit Symphony, was balanced with pieces from antiquity and several nouveau or novel contemporary selections by composers chosen from local university music societies.

Mrs. Grant, a widow, greeted Mr. Samovitch demurely. The two of them were whispered to secrecy. She moved him past statutes of marble nudity and angelic innocence bespoken of accepted indelicacy.

Situated on a risen piece of land and overlooking Lake St Clair along a boulevard gave such grandeur to Grant's house. Built in Edwardian architecture, many porticoes extended past roof areas and buttress's slanted to give solidity to a house built by Albert Kahn at turn of century and listed in many publications. Samovitch was placed in a private end suite with piano and room for staging.

From his window a garden escaped into seclusion. It was walled with benches scattered beneath arbors and vines, During his stay, conductor interviewed and welcomed visiting musicians. Mrs Grants niece clung to her violin and bow with intimacy. Samovitch knew she was of mediocre talent, but invited her to play on end-seating with other orchestra regulars.

An air of Dickens scene collected around all activity during the visit.

Contrasted to this event was an unheralded rock and roll concert in a stadium near Orchestra Hall. No one spoke of Kid Rock's antics, except for younger people who preferred his venues.

The Transcendental Property of Being: Day 55

Glad To Keep Away From Them

She is a wacko.

Totally disassociated from reality.
So far away from right thinking.

She mails me her tax stuff for years I finished.
She includes her social security cards, which I never need nor asked for.

I realized, long ago - over twenty five years past, that she was crazy.

When she used to bring her tax information to me, she would want to rub my back and touch me. I had to tell her to not do that.

The reason I felt sorry for her was that she lost her only son to a gun shot in Detroit and I did his last tax return. I thought her situation was so tragic that I wanted to help her. To this day, she still tells me she goes to the cemetery to pray for him and put flowers on his grave. I cannot even imagine how I could ever deal with such a terrible event (should it ever happen to me).

These things that make up her life, make her disconnected. She actually flirted with me when my wife was sitting next to me.

Once, I felt sorry for her and I assembled a book case that came in a box. I came back from the hardware store with the last part I needed and, in that short space of one half an hour, she had loaded the bookcase and put the television on top of it. I explained to her that I had the part, but she had covered the place where the part went, so I threw away the part and let her live with her half-finished book case.

I never, **never** touched her, because I feared that she would cling like crazy to me. I bought her a television and she never thanked me, but her nutty daughter came over and connected it to her cable. The daughter had no right, but there it was, she took over without talking to me and the two of them went their merry way ignoring me.

Her taxes only took $100 for me to do. She always paid me. Her daughter, over a period of ten years, cheated me out of over $2, 500 and never paid me.

I am not sure how people like her and her daughter make their way through life, but I am so glad to keep away from them.

The Transcendental Property of Being: Day 56

Kindness

Nothing will be as it was.

When things return, normal will be different.
In history, when upheavals occurred,
what restarted was different than before.

God created universe and world,
but Satan upset all orderliness.

It took some time for God to appoint
archangel Michael to restore peace.

Afterwards, contention set in between good
and evil forces. Everything had become upset.

It is a universal truth that change brings with it a new change.
Maxim: The only thing constant on the earth is change.
As a divorced person,
I no longer was what I was as a single person.

I became cautious and careful with all my relationships.
I raised my standards because of what I went through
in my previous marriage.

For those of us who survive the virus sweeping global situations, we will be a little more careful washing our hands or how we touch things. We will be reticent to touch our face. We no longer will simply run our hands over railings or door jambs, but we will step back and take notice of our behavior. It is a common reaction such as avoiding streets where we encountered danger.

When I drive my car, I go slower and stay over to the right lane. I become forgiving to people who get slightly lost or who make last minute decisions to change lanes or make turns without using their turn signals.

I believe that evolution depends upon species adjusting to demanding situations.

But, I will tell you this: Our intrinsic values remain staunch. We who were kind will remain kind. We will only become kinder because of our experiences.

We will avoid all unkind individuals,
as much as possible.

Michael Thomas

The Transcendental Property of Being: Day 57

So Many Souls Waiting

We were working with god, cleaning up the main meeting hall where creation, weddings, funerals and judgements took place.

God was wearing dungarees bib overalls with no t-shirt and splatters of paint were splotched across his back and onto his salt-n-pepper black hair.

He was smoking a cigarette flicking ashes on floor and into a paint can. People kept telling him smoking was bad and he kept repeating that he did not give a damn, he was god and would f___ing do what he wanted.

For some reason, he had a Venus number two soft lead pencil with a worn down eraser, wedged behind his left ear above the ringlet pierced earing. A faded tattoo of archangel Michael spread out over his shoulder, sword drawn, cascading down to his elbow. It was impressive but did not cover over his flabbiness. He was a bit overweight and a half filled bottle of Molson Lager stuck out of his right pocket. A squished pack of Camel cigarettes poked from another pant pocket. The hall was a real mess with paint boards and torn pieces of paper mixed in with a lot of short two by fours.

We continuously kept putting stuff into black trash bags and a crew took them out to a flat-bet truck size of an army deuce and half. Exhaust smoke curled from the muffler pipe. Somebody was playing a cassette recording of Taj Ma Hall singing:

"I pulled out of Pittsburgh an I rolling down the
eastern seaboard

I've got my diesel wound up and she's running like she never did before

There's a speed zone ahead all right, I don't see a cop in sight
Six days upon the road and I gotta see my baby tonight
I got ten forward gears and a sweet Georgia overdrive
I'm taking little white pills and my eyes are open wide
Just passed a Jimmy and a White, I've been passing everything in sight

Six days upon the road and I gotta see my baby tonight
It seems like a month since I kissed my baby bye bye
I got a lot of woman but I'm not like some of the guys
Got my air horns running clear

Baby you oughta watch the way I shift my gears
Six days upon the road and I gotta see my baby tonight
ICC is checking on down the line

Honey you know I'm a little overweight and my log books way behind "

Michael Thomas

But nothing bothers a soul at night, I can dodge them scales all right

Six days upon the road and I gotta see my baby tonight
My rigs a little old but it don't mean she's slow
There's a good flame coming from her smokestack and the smoke's black as coal

My home town coming in sight, if you think I'm happy baby baby baby your right

Six days upon the road and I gotta see my baby tonight."
God kept spitting on dusty trash filled floor.

Outside a line of people waited on folding chairs drinking bottled water.

They were rehearsing their explanations for a final reckoning. Some acne face kids were passing out Seventh Day Adventist "Awake" pamphlets or Gideon bibles as well as selling wrapped candy bars.

The surreal scene had wood statutes of cigar store Indians placed in between chairs as well as weather-worn Blessed Mother figurines barefoot and stepping on snakes. An occasional Saint Francis statute with a cowl headpiece held a birdbath dried up with chirping blue jays flapping around. This was heaven as imagined. People kept warning that a forming group of clouds foretell rain. Every thing was overlaid with mothers breast feeding crying babies. Some held nipple bottles of formula onto their child's sucking mouths. Rumors of Satan appearing, were rampant.

I kept busy reading a tattered copy of Long Day's Journey Into Night by Eugene O'Neill. Some persons read outdated issues

of Sports Illustrated or National Geographic's with their covers ripped off.

I was getting impatient. An angel wandered between us trying to give comfort. One angel kept telling her co-worker that she had never seen so many souls waiting.

The Transcendental Property of Being: Day 58

Dreams

I try so hard to believe in you
Things you do just make me blue
We are worlds apart from things true
And it is no use to try believing in you
When night covers over my dreams
In darkness worlds break their seams
And golden luster has lost its gleam
And it is no use to try believing what seems
I left tomorrow in hazy dust bins
Where good and evil erase all sins
I try so hard to understand all things

But it's no use to try believing what brings
I will be the same today as in a future lie
In broken thoughts I am too sad to cry
For sorrow has left me out to dry
And it's no use to understand why
You will never be different than today
Your sadness will cover all you say
A dark cloud follows you every day
And it's useless to hope or even pray
It is no use to look for dreams to go away

The Transcendental Property of Being: Day 59

Drink Deep

We all want to feel good.
Overcome pain's aging process.
It is easy to understand how addiction can set in.
Throughout history societies have been laced with drugs to
keep populations from agony.

The Yanomami Indians in South America,
shot hullucigens into their nose through a tube.

Old war like groups, gave their soldiers
Marijuana after battle as a reward for killing so well.

The normal process of evolution stages itself
in birth and death.

Death can be viewed as final or continuing.
Tibetan Book Of The Dead is based upon death
and afterlife being similar.

The gauge of similarity
is often based upon awareness levels of each person.

First level is total awareness of all past, present and future lives. In this situation one is freed from reincarnation, Second level is awareness of the immediate life. Third level is no awareness but simply doing what is called floating or drifting from one existence to another with periods of days in between each life,

Suicides are induced to sleep when they pass through the veil. They are given all time needed and awoken only when they can face the fact that they are immortal and that they need to recreate their life to reach a similar point where they do not commit suicide but progress past their despondency.

Bob Dylan has a line in one of his songs: "People don't live or die, people just float."

It is good to remember that no one understands what life is. Did some god make us to search and conjecture through words, art, music, science and all endeavors?

Religion is a panacea for not understanding. It is easy to profess a belief in Jesus, Buddha, Mohammad, Confucius or local TV evangelists.

But, for those of us who pass over these levels, we are left with so many questions that lead to other questions.
The bible is affirmed or refuted by the Essene dead sea scrolls. The dead sea scrolls are backed against ancient tablets and oral traditions such as the Pyramid Texts or Epic of Gilgamesh, including Iliad and Odyssey - first great books of our world by Homer.

The person who gives up on thinking, lives in a bubble of fantasy.

I turn to Thomas Gray who says: Where ignorance is bliss, / Tis folly to be wise."

Alexander Pope says:

"Drink deep, or taste not the Pierian spring"

There shallow draughts intoxicate the brain, and drinking largely sobers us again.

The Transcendental Property of Being: Day 60

In My Care

Isaiah 43:1

But now, this is what the LORD says-- he who created you, O Jacob, he who formed you, O Israel: "Fear not, for I have redeemed you; I have summoned you by name; you are mine. When you pass through the waters, I will be with you; and when you pass through the rivers, they will not sweep over you.

Rabbi Schlotz:

But now we part. You are the strength of my sinews.
You have intellect, wisdom, discretion in all things sacred.
For your benefit, I close my eyes and see you on the mountain before the Lords banquet. I watch as you break bread and drink wine of such supplication that all heaven kneels before you.

But now I will be with you for all time. I will stand silent as you sing to the forest and oceans. I will give you up to light of stars blinking just for you. I will be your servant.

When storms besiege you, I will calm winds. Turn rivers back to their origins. Here in the headsprings of happiness, I will rush you down tears of joy. There I will name you Osiris beneath stones of pyramids.

Beneath fingers of Sphinx my heart will rest upon your wishes. Oh Israel rejoice for you are above all eternities. As cycles fade, you will remain ageless in my care

The Transcendental Property of Being: Day 61

Surviving Mayhem

I decided long ago that Biden was worth being president of us. I made a decision upon Donald Trump being a huckster, snake oil salesman with no value whatsoever. He never loves his neighbor and it is only a bad scene with him.

Because politics falls below poetic insights, I place it in low importance.

We can turn to Galileo Galilei for inspiration in defying the inquisition: As they carted him away to jail, he said to the judges: In the morning, the earth will still turn around the sun.

Of primary importance is a belief in each of us having control over our existence through reincarnation. There is only a heaven or hell for believers who drift or float through life: They have forfeited their vote for reason and given themselves over to irrationality,

We are secure in observing nature in all of its sacred and seemingly profane dramas.

We have ultimate faith that all universes have space for us refugees, away from ignorance.

In shadows of history, we quietly watch as soldiers of malice either pass over us or turn their violence toward us. Our strength is in our submission to a higher calling than sensationalism.

Amen! To all you in the catacombs or caves of invisibility, for you shall survive over mayhem.

The Transcendental Property of Being: Day 62

Evocation Of Anger

A folded note rested on a cold steel bench
that he no longer could feel through all the padding.

Terse words repeated themselves in his mind
as he stared into oblivion.

"Number 2 wants to destroy you. Do not let him."
No signature but only initials. Letterhead bespoke
a power of University of Michigan insignia.

He often wondered where images leave off
and pure violence secured itself onto walls
of his brain like magnets or riveted plates.

He was an offensive tackle facing a defensive end.
His job was to hold a position
so that the play could unfold around him.

He never gave into flights of fancy after running out of a
corridor leading to over one hundred thousand cheering fans
sending an echo like lions roaring unchained.

A coin was tossed. A select group of players rushed into
position facing each other in a bullfight attitude of silence.

They waited for a signal from a quarterback in order to firm their legs and arms in rigidity.

One can never quite imagine those faces of metal. Their grim eyes and pursed lips fell into relief like cave paintings or pictures of boxers who were felled and rising to stand and come into attention for another pounding.

Their profiles were like copies
of Achilles or Ajax, warriors, cut into marble.

Paris let his fingers tingle Helen's skin as she murmured. He depended upon his brothers and fellow soldiers to make up the difference between his effeminate nature
and their ox like natures.

His father, King Priam,
loved him equal to his son, Hector and all his fighters.

Helen loved him for an idea of violence clothed in gentleness. His brother kneeled on a field of battle as sweat formed through a forehead hidden under a helmet of padding.

University of Michigan facing Ohio State became a backdrop to this one-on-one contest waiting for the snap of an odd shaped football called the pig-skin.

Throughout history, civilizations rose and fell under cloaked war . In Homer's words of Greeks facing Trojans.

All these cascading profiles mimicked themselves for this one moment of a cheering crowd. It was like Romans anticipating lions to rip Christians apart in an amphitheater. It was as barbaric contestants poised with swords held tight.

He waited for the impact as his equal pushed against his resistance just as a ball handler stepped back and released a ball tossed to a receiver - all depending upon our hero creating a stand-still,
old and beautiful
as two rhinos
caught in evocation
of anger.

The Transcendental Property of Being: Day 63

My Grandmother Anna

I remember my grandmother as
Fat and simple like a mathematical equation.
Loved Perry Cuomo record she played over and over.
Made her own soap with lye.

Made fresh bread, oven,
flipped the loaves over and over
with a large wood spatula pizza peel.

The sound of the oven doors opening
and closing as the bread cooked.

You can never take away her babushka.

Michael Thomas

She never replaced the large apron she wore over all the time. When we went along a fence lined on a deserted alley, we would pick grape leaves and fill them in her apron she held up like a bag.

I would follow her. I smoked Lucky Strike cigarettes. She would yell at me. Her voice went straight into my heart, Grandma came from the old country. She never spoke English. She was forced to marry a handsome rich man who deserted her immediately. Their marriage was made to join two vineyards. He would come home at night and gave her nine children but never stayed for breakfast.

He married a beautiful nurse and he called for my grandma as he was dying.

She waved him off saying: He never stayed with me and let him die alone.

The bond between this ancient woman of the Earth and myself was strong. I loved her for who she was - a peasant. It was the grape arbor she built hanging over our back yard. It gave shade and fruit. She taught me to plant. She taught me to wait for things to grow.

Her patience was paramount She represented a civilization from past history.

The Transcendental Property of Being: Day 64

Oats of Wisdom

I do not write love poetry anymore.

A decision based upon: Love poetry is self-indulgent for
wanting someone to love me.   It is egotistical.
I have learned to love myself and to no longer yearn for
physical contact or sex to fulfill my desires.

My new inner workings are for more and more information
and new books, music or all things related
to nature and science.

This spiritual depth that engulfs me is not new. It is a
progressive step process of interchanging disciplines that
focus on consciousness rather than the appetites.

It is hard to talk about this because I do not want to be
accused of making more of myself than that I am worth.
Our self-knowledge is all that matters to our judgments.
We are not judged by the amount of orgasms or love poems.

We can only be weighed by our fullness of understanding.
We are like horses and our feed bags nourish us
with oats of wisdom.

Michael Thomas

The Transcendental Property of Being: Day 65

Endless Majesty

To all of you who have not filed your tax return yet, too bad. Remember Joseph and Mary rode a donkey to reach Bethlehem and pay theirs.

Their family health insurance did not cover pregnancy so they had to give birth to Jesus in a straw manger. Old straw that still had animal urine smell.

Shepherds who kept watch over their sheep, cast the "I Ching" using sticks.

The bottom line was voices coming out of the sky. It gave them pause. They tipped the bladder bag up and drank a little more wine.

Eventually, they picked some of their children to keep watch while they walked into town to check out a newborn baby who was supposed to save the Jews who were looking for release of their bondage from the Romans.

These peoples were called the "Essenes" and they kept their story sealed in clay pots buried near the Dead Sea. Eventually archeologists would catch up to them and hire professors to translate these brittle scroll fragments.

Nothing in history comes easy. Tablets of Gilgamesh had to be hosed down - sprayed, to keep them from deteriorating. Even then, Inanna, Utu, Enki and Isimud had to depend upon people they paid to write their story. They got no royalties. Homer lived in a cave with no heat. He did not write the Iliad and Odyssey. He sat cross-legged and recited the two books over and over for all who had time to listen.   Eventually "Speakers" went about the known world giving recitations of both books until Guttenberg invented the printing press with movable typesetting.

There were a lot of rumors that the churches would loose their grip on believers. Because most insignificant people could now have a book to read, forces in control could no longer charge for speaking engagements.

Jesus used a bullhorn for his great Gettysburg Address. Fourscore and seven years ago our fathers brought forth a continent covered with pristine forests and meadows of butterflies and wasps.

Abandon all hope ye who enter this valley of the damned. Give it up. No tears or pleading can ever save you from the devils who collect souls of tearful corpses.

If you were lucky and had some coins called obols to pay a ferryman to carry you across river Styx.

It was a "rum- go" or queer thing to experience dead souls screaming to be pulled out of the desecrated waters of this fetid infamous river.

Michael Thomas

Seven or nine layers of hells circles depicted by Dante in the Inferno: Limbo / Lust / Gluttony / Greed / Anger / Heresy / Violence / Fraud / Treachery.

These were better than the Ten Commandments; certainly more vivid or realistic than:

I am the Lord thy Gold, thou shalt not have any strange gods before me.

Thou shalt not take the name of the Lord thy God in vain.

Remember to keep holy the Sabbath day.

Honor thy father and mother.

Thou shalt not kill.

Thou shalt not commit adultery.

Thou shalt not steal.

Thou shalt not bear false witness against thy neighbor.

Thou shalt not covet thy neighbor's wife.

Thou shalt not covet thy neighbor's goods.

Áve María, grátiā plḗna,
Dóminus tḗcum.
Benedícta tū in muliḗribus,
et benedíctus frū́ctus véntris túī, Iḗsūs.11
Sā́ncta María, Mā́ter Déī,
ṓrā prō nṓbīs peccātṓribus,
nunc et in hṓrā mórtis nóstrae. Āmēn.

Hail Mary, full of grace,
the Lord is with thee.
Blessed art thou amongst women,
and blessed is the fruit of thy womb, Jesus.
Holy Mary, Mother of God,
pray for us sinners,
now and at the hour of our death. Amen.

Got it?

Our Father, who art in heaven,
hallowed be thy Name,
thy kingdom come,
thy will be done,
on earth as it is in heaven.
Give us this day our daily bread.
And forgive us our trespasses,
as we forgive those
who trespass against us.
And lead us not into temptation,
but deliver us from evil.
For thine is the kingdom,
and the power, and the glory,
for ever and ever. Amen.

Michael Thomas

Then there is **The Apostle's Creed**:

I believe in God, the Father Almighty, Creator of Heaven and earth; and in Jesus Christ, His only Son Our Lord,
Who was conceived by the Holy Spirit, born of the Virgin Mary, suffered under Pontius Pilate, was crucified, died, and was buried.
He descended into Hell; the third day He rose again from the dead;
He ascended into Heaven, and sitteth at the right hand of God, the Father almighty; from thence He shall come to judge the living and the dead.
I believe in the Holy Spirit, the holy Catholic Church, the communion of saints, the forgiveness of sins, the resurrection of the body and life everlasting.

Then there is the **Nicene Creed**:

I believe in one God,
the Father, the Almighty,
Maker of heaven and earth,
of all things visible and invisible.
I believe in one Lord Jesus Christ,
the only-begotten Son of God,
born of the Father before all ages,
God from God, Light from Light,
true God from true God,
begotten, not made,
consubstantial with the Father.
Through him all things were made.
For us and for our salvation
he came down from heaven:by the power of the Holy Spirit was incarnate of the Virgin Mary,

and became man.
For our sake he was crucified under Pontius Pilate;
he suffered death and was buried,
and rose again on the third day
in accordance with the Scriptures.
He ascended into heaven
and is seated at the right hand of the Father.
He will come again in glory to judge the living and the dead,
and his kingdom will have no end.
I believe in the Holy Spirit, the Lord, the giver of life,
who proceeds from the Father and the Son.
With the Father and the Son he is adored and glorified.
He has spoken through the Prophets.
I believe in one, holy, catholic and apostolic Church.
I confess one baptism for the forgiveness of sins,
and I look forward to the resurrection of the dead,
and the life of the world to come.

The Magnificat

My soul proclaims the greatness of the Lord,
my spirit rejoices in God my Savior
for he has looked with favor on his lowly servant.
From this day all generations will call me blessed:
the Almighty has done great things for me,
and holy is his Name.
He has mercy on those who fear him
in every generation.
He has shown the strength of his arm,
he has scattered the proud in their conceit.
He has cast down the mighty from their thrones,
and has lifted up the lowly.
He has filled the hungry with good things,

and the rich he has sent away empty.
He has come to the help of his servant Israel
for he remembered his promise of mercy,
the promise he made to our fathers,
to Abraham and his children forever.

It is almost too much, but here goes one of my most favorites:

Tantum ergo Sacramentum
Veneremur cernui:
Et antiquum documentum
Novo cedat ritui:
Praestet fides supplementum
Sensuum defectui.
Genitori, Genitoque
Laus et jubilatio,
Salus, honor, virtus quoque
Sit et benedictio:
Procedenti ab utroque
Compar sit laudatio. Amen.

Down in adoration falling,
Lo! the sacred Host we hail,
Lo! o'er ancient forms departing
Newer rites of grace prevail;
Faith for all defects supplying,
Where the feeble senses fail.
To the everlasting Father,
And the Son Who reigns on high
With the Holy Spirit proceeding
Forth from each eternally,
Be salvation, honor blessing,
Might and endless majesty. Amen.

The Transcendental Property of Being: Day 66

Modern Psalm

Big man,
Big woman,
Put me into your big Rolls Royce and give me wine.
I will eat whole cashews and look out
the window at passing scenes.

Dear never dying circles; surround me like hula hoops.
I am skipping rope and keeping time with your boom box.
For holiday garnish I will sprinkle hallucinogenic mushrooms
ground up like salt over my chicken gumbo.

Dear galactic leader; let me land my space ship
in one of your car ports.
I will pay the parking meter.

Before lights go out, I will rise above clamor and mayhem.
I will give the signal to the announcer to begin my prayer.
Holy, holy, holy God and all his production managers.
I watch the monitor for a clue to your resurrection.
My heart is sore for benefice.

I wish all who ever knew me,
to find a peace within your hearts.
And I spread my hands in grace over the multitudes who left
the banquet with a small piece of wisdom from my words.

Michael Thomas

The Transcendental Property of Being: Day 67

I am Appreciative

It is confusing how I love.
I have, first, always loved a god.
Second, I have loved myself.

I married a woman whom I did not love.
My profession was that I would learn to love her.
That never came about. I could not stand even living with her.

She was never treated cruelly/ Our sex was gentle.
When I left her, after five years, I paid all my support and saw the teo children all the time.

After her, I lived with my second intimate partner.
That situation ended after three years. I carried hurt for over seven more years.

I lived, for a following thirty five years, in a relationship with a woman who had a loving husband. I had no sex with her, but gave time and all my energy to keep her in my graces. She died and since then, I have been given back all monies and feelings of self-satisfaction.

I never seemed to get over my second love. She only just appeared in my dreams and here is the quandary presented:

She and her sister were my lovers and we were buying a new house for the three of us to live in.

A house with space for two families. This house was so snug and comfortable, attractive to us all. It was mentioned how the house had no bad smells in or outside of it.

My big question was whether we were going to expand things to make one living space. A common house with all three of us doing the cleaning and cooking seemed so pleasing.

Then I awoke with reality setting in.

My waking thoughts were: That I have never been cruel or mean with all the people I have loved. That is a given and I remain a gentle person with a distinctly separate partner in business for over thirty years and a large group of clients. I am a rich and painless person with good health for over eighty years. I am fortunate enough to have over twenty books published.

It seems like I have been given so much and I am appreciative.

The Transcendental Property of Being: Day 68

Abnormalities

There is a consciousness aside from our consciousness.
A world apart from our world

A place where our beliefs get extended past what we believe. In order to reach this space, we need to clear ourselves of ego. We must move past all we know of who we are.

I remember when I returned from Hong Kong and stepped up to my entrance to my barracks in Vietnam. I experienced a sudden realization that I did not know who I was and I did not recognize this as my home or life.

It was not that I did not want to be where I was: It was just that something different existed and I did not know what it was.

I have experienced this disassociation at various times in my life.

Once when I was pitched high by swimming, bicycling and running marathons. I had reached a level of extraordinary awareness,. I totally remembered I spoke to myself that I could not leave my body at that exact moment because I still had many things to complete with all my associations and responsibilities.

At one point in being high on drugs, I was driving in a convertible car going toward the Rocky Mountains. We had reached a point when the huge horizon opened to elevations beyond my imagination,. I said to my companion: Please grab me because I am going to leave my body,. My feeling was that a force coming from afar was trying to pull me out of myself. My companion held my shoulder and I stayed inside myself.

I am not bragging and I have known something different about me that others did not share.

I will tell you what it is: It is like a person shadowing me that knew all about me but waited in the background for a time when I would fade and that person would become prominent. To have this awareness is not a detriment to my existence. I am just a normal person with abnormalities.

We all have these anomalies and it is only when present conditions cannot hold back these situations, which they surge forward and take hold of us.

The Transcendental Property of Being: Day 69

Jew

We did not chose
To be Jews
'Yesterday's news'
Lined up in pews
Chanting blues

Mamma they're pushing us
Making such a fuss
Nobody we can trust
Smoke extinguishes
No time to discuss

We are left overs
Roll over rovers
There's a story here
Realizing our fear
Can a god hear?

Clogged up gear
Rotisserie speared
Last of our tears
Days turn to years

A German democracy
Turned into mockery

Losing proprietary
How easy we burn
It is our turn
In ovens of sacrifice

We give up our lives
All we can do is hope and pray
That these memories go away

Michael Thomas

The Transcendental Property of Being: Day 70

As We Breathe

I have incense spread around my rooms in a balm of essence,. It keeps bugs away. Rodents think of it as smoke from a fire. Fire indicates danger to their instincts,.

When I moved into my house, living conditions of the previous occupants precipitated flies which took about three years to rid themselves from the crevices near windows or vents.

To me, it is strange that people live unclean. Smells coming from my neighbors apartments often irritate me. Each person has their own levels of tolerance for cooking or odors inside their rooms. My grit has always been tight for purity and during church services; my favorite was when acolytes swung censors infusing burning frankincense into mysticism of prayer and reverence.

Walks through woods are always accompanied with the musty drift of decaying forest leaf and fungus. These smells evoke a wild untamed feeling inside me. I can remember poking my walking stick to turn over deceased furry creatures and catching a whiff of deaths exhumation.

Ocean or lake breezes carry a moisture of evaporation smells like dead fish or algae. These create an image of life in stages. Feelings of differentiation would pass through me as I removed hooks from fish and threw their slimy skinned scales back into water to give them another chance at life.

That is our story: Smells bring us a picture of birth and death that consumes us all as we breathe.

The Transcendental Property of Being: Day 71

Good luck My Friend

It seems to me Jesus did not have Chap Stick or a cell phone. His dad was a carpenter, so they may have had grit materials to sand down rough edges of sawed wood. If they did they could have used what they had to trim down their toenails or fingernails.

Mother of Jesus probably gave him a haircut.

Jesus told his schoolmates: Someday we will have Gillette triple edge blade razors. Until then, keep your beard trimmed and free of food particles

"Be sure to use skin of pig intestines for safe sex. I have seen how Mary Magdalene checks you out,.."

In the future you will have a bible to read from Gideon's. Until then, just keep struggling with parchment copies of Dead Sea Scrolls. There is not too much need for "letters to editors". You will have a lot of people writing about you along with Napoleon, Alexander the great and Buddha.

Believe half of what you hear and none of which you read. Jews escaping from Pharaoh will lead to Moses being given Ten Commandments burnt into stone tablets, twice. Moses finally wore gloves, they were very hot and he dropped them at first. Remember to Honor Thy Father And Mother.

We do not believe what they are saying about you wandering around the Dead Sea with twelve men being gay. You could dispel such stories by claiming marriage to Magdalene. Take blood tests for her children.

"When I find myself in times of trouble, mother Mary comes to me speaking words of wisdom, let it be, let it be."

Newspaper accounts of you being the Messiah may or may not be true. There are a lot of false prophets making that claim all through the ages. It was conjectured that Simon of Cyrene was questioned by Pontius Pilate and he answered affirm that he was. Pontius was confused because his wife told him that you, Jesus, was in India studying words of Buddha.

Be careful how you use your powers. Lazarus denounces you since he now has to die all over again. When Lazarus came back, his sisters made him set table, wash dishes and take out garbage. He was not very happy to have to defend himself a second time for sexual misbehavior.

I know how hard it is to walk around dusty roads getting your feet dirty. Try L.L. Bean Duck Boots.

I am Jesus, son of god
Pass me up, with a nod
People following are photographers
They want many sermons, lectures
What I say has been said before
Love your neighbor at your door
Give forgiveness a positive chance
A handshake or at the point of a lance
Good luck, my friend.

The Transcendental Property of Being: Day 72

Thinking Outside A Box

Mabel had fenced in areas.

Spike, a white creature size of a gerbil had no tail or fur. It was like a sausage and its eyes were hidden by slight skin covering.

When I was visiting, Spike jumped over his fence and boldly walked up to a neighbor he knew who begin to feed him eating out of his fingers.

I asked Mabel: Why a fence? Oh! Spike likes to exercise and he appreciates limits that he can overcome like he is in training for Olympics that never will happen.

Will Spike get lost?

Mabel: No. He always comes back from his junctures.

Do other animals in other cages all get out?

Mabel: Yea. I make sure each one has an outlet and they all come back.

Me to Mabel: I would never let you be my zoo keeper.

Michael Thomas

Maybe life is similar to your cages. We all like boundaries but when we leave them to explore, we come back to safety.

I remember a saying: *"Everyone is a hero or famous except in their home."*

Partial lyrics from a song: "Little Boxes" by Malvina Reynolds:

> And the people in the houses
> All went to the university,
> Where they were put in boxes
> And they came out all the same,
> And there's doctors and lawyers,
> And business executives,
> And they're all made out of ticky-tacky
> And they all look just the same.

Great people in history, Vasco da Gama, Ferdinand Magellan, Christopher Columbus - They all returned from their explorations. Carl Jung berated Sigmund Freud for never considering information past his premise of life before birth or reincarnation. Freud refused thinking past Id, Ego, Superego.

Muhammad always returned to his wife, Maymunah bint al-Harith and kept giving her more children.

Leo Tolstoy would come home to his wife, Sophia Tolstaya, and she kept rewriting his book: War and Peace, as it changed. She also kept the estate functioning orderly while he was away.

Isaac Newton never could reconcile his fellow students at Trinity College who drank and partied their time away, while he assiduously studied as he made his discoveries. He was confounded by their wasting so much time frivolously,

Mary lost Jesus and found him preaching to elders at such an early age, and Jesus told her: *"Do you not know that I must be about my father's business?"*

I guess we all like overcoming limitations. Alexander The Great wrote to his mother how he hated being so far away from home and her.

I remember as a footloose traveler I relished returning to my mother and father for a much needed rest.

Such a condition did not mean that I reverted to an earlier way of thinking. It just meant that my learning needed closure by tying loose ends in a manner of revisiting my beginnings. Life is funny. Life is never black and white. World histories do not progress along straight lines. There are always junctures and Sydney J. Harris, 1917 to 1986, proclaimed that he came upon novel thinking by following outside main topics of research,. He went where leads led him.

We all do the same by thinking outside a box.

The Transcendental Property of Being: Day 73

Back Forth

Sadness to empty stores:
Malls all shut down.
Not one car in a parking lot.
Not one face, to peek at you out of corner of eyes.

Pathos of people separated from each other with
Masks hiding faces.

Fear of a virus that kills our overpopulation.
Cars not being driven.
Streets with no traffic.
Traffic lights so desolate for a purpose.
Air clean from no car smog.
Churches, on Easter morning,
With not one car and all doors closed.

We are not meant to be divided from one another.

We are social animals that built our world together.
We are meant to touch,
Have love passed hand to-mouth-to shoulder pats.

When this virus has ended, will be better for it?
Will we appreciate paths of friendship between us?

When we emerge from caves of our isolation?
Will we learn to decrease our angers
And search for answers to life-death
That step over old boundaries?

When Satan was thrown out of heaven,
Last thing he did was turn,
Look back and shed a tear that god saw.
They waved, and blew kisses back-forth.

Michael Thomas

The Transcendental Property of Being: Day 74

Being Judged Unfairly

I came under suspicion for effeminacy.

Being subtlety accused in a
quiet snide manner embarrassed me.

Family members of Grace
inferred my intentions were underhanded.

Of course, I was attracted to her.
They were simply being over protective.

I had been seen packing a sewing bag of needle,
thread and other assorted sewing paraphernalia
like scissors and an embroidery hoop.

My items were placed in a handmade denim satchel
with a change of clothing.

As a man, my family were disappointed that I never played
sports. I always leaned toward books and spiritual erudition.
To them I was under a cloud of being gay
despite my masculine physique.

Grace had a sister. Both of them were favored by their
physician father and educated mother. Both of them secretly

sneered at me. I was pictured as lower caste to them. Maybe
I was, because I had not come into my future status. I was
sort-of a Dumbo and open to ridicule.

They made fun of my not knowing a current singer,
without them understanding
that I preferred classical music above all others.

It is too bad that we all grow or mature at different levels.
The disparity between us all gives issue for fitness
under circumstances.

I will tell you this: If early on I was a wrong fit for Grace and
her sister, as time ensued, I surpassed their divorce and
schooling deficits.

I simply turned into a better person
who was being judged unfairly
by standards that no longer applied to me.

The Transcendental Property of Being: Day 75

Inside Devotions Of Dancing

Fluidity of cello, violin, violincello:
String quartets of Haydn flow together
in sequential embodiment.

Haydn steps toward Mozart and Beethoven in simple
repetition of understandable meanings.
String quartet instruments talk to each other
like call/response.

A basic pattern in music is dance. When we listen to feet, arm
swinging in Baroque mannerism we can imagine glowing
chandeliers cascading down over proper movements;
a ceremony of light gaiety with puppet like precision.
The string quartet is magical without heaviness
of orchestral entanglement.

Symbiotic swaying leaves us entangled gracefully.

Our minds are freed from darkness
and deep symphonic statements.

How we twirl
Lacey swirl
We give up our resistance
For opportunist insistence
Close our eyes let instinct take over
For syncopation with our lover

Memory fades with bow and string
Leading us where seasons spring
And our hearts become feathery
In an unburdened wistful brevity

Consciousness opens new paths
Where meadow flowers lapse
Into bouquets within our grasp
Time condenses into synapses

And fingers cling to a fantasy
Of a shared partner of destiny
Love is a motion of floating
Inside devotions of dancing

Michael Thomas

The Transcendental Property of Being: Day 76

People Just Float

There is always a tie-in.

We close our stories in our head,
then something changes what we knew.

Fritzie died in Maggie's arms.
He was a bachelor for so long
and he lived with his sister and Hank.

Hank, Maggie and Fritz bought a large house
on elevated land
with twenty three acres on outskirts of Chicago
in Joliet Illinois.

The story revolves around three of them living together
 till Fritzie died of liver problems from his incessant drinking.
The story is that Hank never drank and he lived to an old age
over ninety like his wife lived concurrently till death.
But Fritzie died first.

Story is how Hank and Fritzie competed with each other.
They both bought riding lawn mowers
and would zig zag over the land
avoiding each other as they cut grass.

Story is how Fritzie got so drunk every night and local police would drive him home and tell Maggie where they left Fritzie's pick up.

This is a tale of real people who live their lives with all the associated drama coming out of it.

But here is the twist: Fritzie was given a lot of money to run a drinking club near St Mathias church. Not much was said about Fritzie's life other than he was divorced early and could always be found leaning over the bar asleep. This man had a dark past of losing all monies that came into his possession. He lost everything. He died owing so many people who never bothered coming to his funeral. He died in his sisters arms. He was buried in a grave that no one visited. To the left of his grave lay buried Maggie and Hank's markers.

These are good people embroiled in life's vicissitudes up to their necks.

They built a small basement bar with flashing lights and bottles of liquor in front of a painted mirror. When Fritzie woke, he would sit at the home bar and get drunk before he drove to the club and got further drunk.

Fritzie's trauma was how he felt guilty owing so many people,. Photographs of Fritzie, Hank and Maggie were taped to the back-lit bar mirror.

Years later, when demolition leveled all older vacated buildings, these photos were buried with the rubble.

Michael Thomas

That is where our bodies rest, somewhere in a plot of land as we desiccate in time to polished bones that even physical archaeologists or anthropologists. are not interested in. People who conduct autopsies have a favorite term: "Unremarkable" to describe portions of a body sliced open.. We are unremarkable people living and dying as Bob Dylan says in one of his songs: "People don't live or die, people just float."

The Transcendental Property of Being: Day 77

Faith And Hope Dead

Do not fret
Humanity
Consistently
Intentionally
Places wrong bets
Murder, war
Women's rights
Peasant's plights
Screaming nights
Chaos an open door
We bury history
In such sadness
Redemption-less
Devil's hot kiss
Plagues of misery
Cries for relief
Drift away unheard
Reason is blurred
And, in a word,
Peace is so brief
So, listen, I've said
Pain won't go away
Day after day
Charities grey
Faith and hope dead

Michael Thomas

The Transcendental Property of Being: Day 78

Rest In Peace My Friend

Because I am locked into my home to avoid the virus, I feel the need to talk to you, my clients or listeners.

I am not famous, but I have twenty books published and about three hundred people who I advise or prepare taxes for as a Certified Public Accountant.

I am kind of like Donald Trump, since I like to talk about myself. He is one of the most self-centered persons in public that I have ever seen.

First of all, I have favorite clients. Jay and Piper of Main Street Motors since 1974 are magical married couple. Piper was brought back from the dead because of Jay's prayers. The doctors could not believe her recovery since they wrote her off as dead.

Stephen Willey left Main Street Motors; had an operation and became Stephanie Willey changing his sex to a woman. She now talks in a faintly falsetto voice, but the gruff male intonation still remains.

My next favorite people are Robert and Erica Perry. The IRS put them through hell and they have since risen above that terrible audit with an agent who should be removed from the service. Robert is a landscape artist who has had many jobs over the years. Erica worked for years as a spokesperson for kidney transplant operations in Ann Arbor. The two of them are so happily married that it makes me jealous,

There are so many clients who are kind. The few crooks drop off my radar. One such thief and his wife cheated his way by using workers and he was one of the only one who I saw bribe a government employee. This man cheated me out of over twelve thousand dollars. So long jerk.

Attilla Huth and Sandy Ryder top my list. She sold homemade cheesecakes for years and still runs Wild Swan Theatre doing plays for children. What a wonderful lady Sandy is with her gregarious nature. Attila has a construction company and he builds houses so beautiful.

There have been three or four extremely rich and famous clients who came-and-went. One is now the owner of a company worth over fifty eight million dollars. I do not talk to him because he cheats people to become rich. Another client is a lovely man who became so big that I had to tell him to switch to Arthur Anderson since I refused to leave Ann Arbor and become his worldwide comptroller. A third person was so much part of me becoming a Buddhist. He left the path of spiritually and I left him when he became too famous for words. He also is still on the internet and I wish him well. When I told him to find another CPA, his words were: We go way back. I know how far back we went but we no longer go forward.

I am a blabber. I thank all you who I have not mentioned. Darry Dusbiber who does lighting for movie sets. What a

gentleman and his wife, a retired school teacher, I have a warm spot in my heart for them.
It is funny, when you have so many clients, the thought of them pops into my head and then pops out.

I will tell you a funny story. I assembled all my books to send to my ex-wife and I stopped dead. I suddenly remembered writing stories of her in a not too kind fashion. I do not think she will ever read any of my books but I do not want to put any more logs on the fire of her hatred toward me. To this day, I do not know what she hates me for, other than I disavowed her and broke my promise to marry her till death do we part. Over fifty percent of marriages end up in divorce, I think is the ratio.

One of my best loved clients is a professor in New York at Columbia. I find his lectures on You Tube and watch avidly as he espouses his trips into the jungles to draw information for his Anthropology work.

Three piano players now run the music departments in three Universities in the country. I do their taxes and adore their music since I am a die-hard classical music lover. I have three external hard drives full of all the orchestral, string music in the world.

I talk too much and I feel so fortunate to have known one woman for over thirty years who guided my life. Pamela is dead, as well as her husband. She was an adept who could heal. She was a confident, who identified flowers on our nature hikes, that has stayed with me. Rest in peace my friend.

The Transcendental Property of Being: Day 79

A Detective Mundane Mystery

She loved Morton Feldman's music.

Detective Sergeant Mundane listened to it in an attempt to tie-in her death.

It was minimalistic repetition similar to Philip Glass. In this investigation there was very little evidence. She was strangled but no fingerprints on her neck. No rope. He maintained the corpse stopping the family from burying her. Dorothy Feinstein was close to getting her degree in chemistry. So much hope evaporated after her death. Her family paid off the last of her student loan and held memorial services constantly,

Detective Mundane went to sleep with beeps and blips of Feldman's "Rothko Chapel"

His secretary stopped him and asked: What is that ridiculous music you are listening to day-after-day? It is like someone put a sock in your mouth to hear your voice,

He was stopped in his thoughts. He rushed back to the evidence locker and looked at every piece in the box, to no avail. He then returned to Dorothy's bedroom letting his eyes flow everywhere and not knowing what he was looking for.

Michael Thomas

He made a phone call to Burt, asking to be sure there were no finger marks on the corpse's neck. Burt did remark that there were small fabric residue.

Mundane swept under the bed with a back scratcher and found a sock. It was a winter wool size large. He put it in a plastic bag.

Driving back to talk to Burt, he absentmindedly listened to Steve Reich and Terry Riley with recurring thoughts of: How simple sounds over and over constituted music.

A body kept frozen was brittle. Burt poked it with a chrome extension,. Mundane asked him to compare the cloth on her sock to her neck.

Burt: "It is a match! I'll be damn. It is a match"

Mundane: "Look for what is on the sock, please."

The court proceedings took little time to convict and sentence Mundane's suspect. Fingerprints matched it was a murder weapon used to strangle Dorothy.

Case closed and Mundane went back to Bach, Mozart as more understandable music. He slept uneasy thinking of Dorothy losing her breath as a sock shut her esophagus from air.

The Transcendental Property of Being: Day 80

Failure Belies Best Intentions

Tao Te Chin written by Lao-Tse, translated by James Legge:

> Always without desire we must be found,
> If its deep mystery we would sound;
> But if desire always within us be,
> Its outer fringe is all that we shall see.

Rabbi Schlotz, writer translated by Michael Thomas:

> We that are bound by propriety
> Shall be loosed by degeneracy
> Those bound by prophecy
> Shall be loosed by heresy
> For future of all our existence
>
> We will die from our insistence
> When truth becomes known
> All of life's lies will be shown
>
> We have been groomed to smile
> But inside our hearts is all guile
> Bird in hand makes us greedy
> For a mansion with an aviary
> Words we speak make all reality

We create worlds with impunity
If I have your total reliance
I shall want total obedience
Let this be your best lessons
Failure belies best intentions

The Transcendental Property of Being: Day 81

Ghosts

Beginning claims for this elevated
piece of property were confused.

Originally an arson fire took log cabin and outdoor privy.
Occupants died instigating a murder case.

A lone drifter rebuilt the cabin and laid claim with a contested
quit-claim deed. He also died and was convicted killer.
Mud covered ash sloped down drainage.

An assessor threw up his hands
and split deeds to create two parcels.

To those who believed in bad spirits were added new owners
who tried to pray away old stories of voodoo. But, late at
night, moaning was carried on a wind moonlit scene.

Eventually drainage pipes were laid.
Roads followed as well as street lights that flickered spookily.

These small sections of land became storefronts
that leaned into each other.

Sounds carried through each wall
and during storms there was a creaking.

Michael Thomas

We often are awakened as if by ghosts that were invisible.
We lived in a second floor apartment
so hidden away that mail did not get to us.

There was a reference insurance attachment addressing a
possible future cost of insulation against night whispering
voices.

Up and down short streets drivers often felt
a shifting of white lines on asphalt,
as well as a knocking of their tires against the friction.
This was manifest in stories titled "knock-knock-street".

We can only compare this to miners who carried stories of
mayhem through their towns

Later in years vacated doorways with burnt out light bulbs
brought terror to my mind
as I walked quickly to pass through these locations.

The Transcendental Property of Being: Day 82

Rage, Rage

You no longer can be a drifter.
No longer can you float.

Make a decision. Take a stand.

If I ask you a question, give me a definite answer.
What kind of music do you like?

Do not say: "I don't know."

I want you to say that you know and you are willing to die for something.

I, first of all, want you to quit smoking cigarettes.
In the short time I sat with you outside, you coughed over twenty five times. That is not acceptable. You are letting cigarettes control you. You are not in a position of monitoring smoking.

General Patton did not take no for an answer. He sent his men roaring straight into enemy territory with their tanks and half-tracks. He cursed to himself these words: "Fuck them. Just go right past their bullets."

Michael Thomas

I will tell you what makes a good commander: They would do just what they ordered their men to do. The best leader leads front and center.

You are not married, but live with a smart woman. She does not smoke or harm herself. By smoking cigarettes you are hurting her, because she is depending upon you staying alive long enough to marry you and have children. What the fuck is wrong with your thinking? You are killing yourself before your children are born,.

Your problem is that you are not acting like General Eisenhower or Caesar. You are letting the opposition defeat you like a wimp. You are exposing your weakness and letting arrows of poison take you down.

I am not happy watching you not watch yourself.
At your age, of twenty five, you are not going to live past fifty. Here is what you need to do: You need to replace one fault with another habit. You need to exchange smoking for something else. Like, maybe, exercise or a task so that one bad venture recedes and another better venture ascends. It is so simple. Sometimes great thinkers simply think like children.

You need to start talking to yourself like you were a two year old.

And, you need to wash your hands more. The grease from your job still hangs on under your fingernails.

I love you like a brother and you are only my neighbor.
If I give you a gift, as I have over-and-over, you need to become effusive with thanks. You are only deserving of what you appreciate.

That is your main problem: You are not thankful for your life and grateful for being young and having hope of marriage with forthcoming children.

I am your punisher and overseer. I am your salvation. Pay attention to me and respect yourself as a buffalo or bison would in wild nature. You cannot roar if you cough like a dead eagle. Your ego is deflated.

Brandon, stop and consider how hateful you are treating yourself. You are better than what you are exhibiting.
Here is what I am going to do: I am going to shove you down on the ground till you realize who you are and what you are capable of.

I am not perfect, but I am over eighty years old and I take care to see a doctor, eat good food, keep my thoughts as pure as possible. I treat the world as my gift and give back to the world all I can in my power.

That is what you need to do: Give back to a world for what a world has given you. As Dylan Thomas says to his father:

"Do not go gentle into that good night
Rage, rage against the dying of the light."

The Transcendental Property of Being: Day 83

Death and Taxes

cautious over future
nothing is sure
cannot rest
life test

in a jungle of banana trees
I have no bananas

efforts toward security
balancing duality
inner and out
I pout

great people of history
challenged their destiny
even their examples
passed down
confuse us

I am only confident of loving my neighbor
even though their cooking smells noxious
their music is raucous
their dog barks
they disdain saying hello to me
I often want to shove them down
till they hit bottom

just to see surprise on their faces
will assure me that I love them
listen: my words mean nothing and any comments
you make will just roll off my back like water on a duck

I have never listened to my ex wife
to this day, she is still a fool
if I was foolish to marry her
I am no longer the fool to have divorced

I have surpassed Catholicism
and all established beliefs
only Buddhism remains
central to reincarnation
doing over-and-over
better than hell
or a heaven
of doldrums

there's a hole in daddies arm where all the money goes
Jesus died for nothing, I suppose (John Prine,
who died April 7, 2020)

Arnold Schwarzenegger: "I'll be back"
Lenny Bruce: If Jesus comes back we will kill him again
Lazarus spit on the ground and faced death over again.
St Peter said: I do not know that man
Jesus was studying in India
He let Simon of Cyrene
   take being hung

History is funny. All we can be sure of is death and taxes

The Transcendental Property of Being: Day 84

She Of All She's

Lady of all ladies - As brilliant as a blue jay
Magnificent as a first star exploding into existence
From out of an inviting sky waiting for luminescence
She stood upon a summit between poles of galaxies

Her arms outstretched like a shirt swinging on a clothesline
in a wind - A trumpet bleated attention

A stillness settled over all expectant mirages
"I am she who came before your ancestors came into form"
Her voice settled echoes from all horizons
"I am she who gives you milk from my breasts of infancy
Let thy lips suck honey molasses juice of myrrh of my
extended nipples"

A moan cascaded across comet traced valleys
of invisible souls.

"I am before I was. I will be after you are gone.
See seats if my present"

There was a rumbling of thunder followed by bolts
of lightning cursing across a startled sky.

There was a threat of rain never arriving within cloud smoked whispering.

"I am what you dream. I am what you dare to never be. I am she who deigns to blossom roses and my thorns shall pierce your fingers as you try to reach for me"

"I am little but larger than your imaginings. I am full and empty of vanity. Calm thyself in my court since I am gracious as an elk on knees of adoration"

The Transcendental Property of Being: Day 85

It Was Apropos

Past and present overlap, at times.
Charlie and his wife, Martha, cheated me out of over twelve thousand dollars.

They were audacious enough to want me as a favorable witness in one of their many lawsuits. Of course, I feigned memory loss and got out of giving them what they wanted. He and his wife stiffed so many people and conducted bribes of official government representatives.

In my dream I was sitting in well decorated offices of statutes and onyx veneered lacquer furniture. I sat across from his wife, who was now a famous attorney. I thanked her for allowing me to assist her and I kept a wary thought about her. She offered drink and confections.
I asked her a subtle question to test her.

"Do you still do work for Reichenbach?"

She answered yes. I left it at that and as I walked out to go to my car, she stopped me. "Why are you going that way? You can get out the other way."

I turned and left but doubled back the other way where I connected her to Charlie's warehouses located in a distance. So, she was still connected to her devious husband as well as now being a barrister.

I got in my car just as another client was pulling up to park. He stuck his head out of window and said hello. Then he said this: "I would appreciate if you do not mention that you are affiliated with me"

I apologized with words to effect that I often blurt out things without thinking. He nodded and we drove away from each other.

My life is complicated. People often consider me lower than them and they often give me less credit for being astute. I think of Tao Te Chin saying that a wise man acts a fool to hide wisdom. It was apropos.

The Transcendental Property of Being: Day 86

You, Tell Me, Please ...

Soren Kierkegaard (1813-1855) postulates three principals of existence: aesthetic, ethical and religious.

I, Rabbi Schlotz, declare there is: my thoughts,
my reflections and god.

As I go through life, in my mind,
I carry on a continuous conversation.

If I wake, I moan as a world fills in slow thoughts
and muscles begin to work again.
This process of coming aware has been with me all my years.

When I drop things, I exclaim,
"Oh! There it is!" as I find it below me.

Banging my fingers by mistake
with an implement arouses an: "Ouch!"

During orgasm sex or seeing a rainbow makes me say:
"Wow! or My god! or Jesus Christ"

Last stages in a natal ward when my contractions are in final stages of dilation delivering, I scream:
Get this fucking thing out of me, please.

No wonder we cling to our children so firmly,
we hate them for putting us through childbirth.

So, this interior mirror-self is well established with all of us.
There is a joke that: Talking to yourself is okay as long as you
do not answer back.

People who talk to themselves are highly proficient and count
on only themselves to figure out what they need, according to
Albert Einstein.

In therapy, questions are asked us that bring forth memories
of how, what, why, when or where we acted.

This makes us two people as well as a third god.

To people who are atheists we can pose the question of
prove you can make a flower from your thoughts.
Only a god or a third spirit can do that.

The magic reality surrounding all of us draws out our awe.
If it does not, then sad for you.

Rene Descartes (1506-1650) says: I am a thing that thinks.

Karl Jung (1875-1961) says: We were before we became.
Jung uses pre-birth language patterns as a method
of proving we exist in life before life.

I am sure a lot of people who get divorced say out loud:
Why, the hell, did I marry that person?

You, tell me, please.

Michael Thomas

The Transcendental Property of Being: Day 87

Mique: Hair-Dresser, Madam, Drug-Dealer, Friend

I never wanted one of Mique's whores.
I just wanted to do her bookkeeping, get my monthly fifty dollars and get out of her warm attic third floor office.
Her and her husband, Bobbie, had weekly parties in their condo with music, drugs and alcohol.
I never wanted any part of that either.

Eventually cops raided and threw everyone in jail.
Eventually the house where she had her beauty salon-bordello was torn down and a high rise put in its place.

Funny, how history moves past issues into dust.
For years, as I would pass where her old house was, I could only imagine it buried beneath this twenty story façade.
Bobby took a job building pallets for a moving company.
He hired Mexicans to staple strips of useless wood
into square frames.

He and Mique moved into a sordid house on an extended part of town where street lights were all shot out and darkness blended in with black squirrels and rodents. Absolutely no light shown threw dark no-curtain windows. It was like a morgue.

I would see their broken down cars parked with the tires all flat in a dirt driveway.

Eventually I visited Mique in the hospital and read poetry to her before she died of cancer. Her daughter was a carbon copy of her - so young and as uneducated. Her daughter was glad to leave to have a cigarette in a non-smoking area of hospital grounds,

Mique held my hand. She had tubes sticking out of her nose, arms and stomach. She was half asleep from intravenous medications. Every one of her party friends or ex-husbands had deserted her and she lay there all alone.

Mique's life was like a sad western novel with a continuing plot of bleak connections. We can only hope for a heaven to give her rest before she comes back to repeat.

I remember reading Carlos Castaneda's book, The Teachings of Don Juan: A Yaqui Way of Knowledge. Castaneda asks the Indian: Who can become a man of knowledge? The Indian points to the rabble of people on the street and tells the student: Anyone of all of these can become a person of knowledge.

I was drawn to Mique as a friend and I never discounted her ability to rise above the conditions she had set for herself and for her to become a person of wisdom. Maybe someday she will read this story about her and realize some absolute truths.

The Transcendental Property of Being: Day 88

A Really Big Cheesy World

I do not remember his name.
He was a widower neighbor old days.
I was young, under twelve.

Why did I go to visit him in the nursing home? I do not know. He cried from having someone thinking about him. He had nobody.

I do remember I took a box of chocolates which he opened. He dribbled eating one. Offered me. I took and thanked. Surprise on peoples face when unexpected things happen. That is what I like best. A heartfelt gratitude. I think it softens their inside soul. I think it is a balm takes away pain for a short time so they can catch their breath and remember that maybe a god does exist and I come to them as some angel agent of divine resemblance.

Virginia McHarg and Eleanor Ladendorf ran De Lasalle's high school library on Connors Avenue across from Detroit City Airport. I could never get enough of their smiles when they greeted me. I shelved their books and kept order for them. They would suggest so many books for me to read. For a small amount of energy expended, I received so much back as an inadvertent reward.

Life is an adventure of people opening their secret doors to me. It was wonderful to experience true love from them.
I was an altar boy who assisted the priest in services. I used to watch faces of people in pews with babushkas covering their shadowed prayer mumblings. Funny how praying was done with murmuring to some invisible god.

Bless me father for I have sinned. Going to confession is like being at an alcoholic AA meeting. Hi, I am Michael and I am an alcoholic. I also have a mother and father who argue so much they wake up neighbors. Let me tell you, when my parents would shout and throw things at walls crashing, it was me who felt guilt that I was causing their distemper.

My uncle would try to intervene between them. He would tell them that you are making the children cry. My dad would say: The hell with children and hell with my god damn wife.
It was so terrible trying to go to sleep with all that fighting. Made me feel like they should have never given me birth. This story has a developing plot that seems to link topics. Here we go to school looking for walnuts. Listening to morning and evening doves coo with so much birdlike devotion.

Here we go stopping at DeBucks bakery and getting a free donut from the jolly lady in a white hat and apron. Here we go passing two barbers standing inside a store window waving to us as we walked to school. These stories are a shortened version of "Remembrance of things past" by Proust or a poem by Dylan Thomas, "The force that through the green fuse drives the flower"

We live as small chunks of things in a really big cheesy world.

Michael Thomas

The Transcendental Property of Being: Day 89

Return To Normal

Two witness requirement for virtual marriage
to Sue and Mark.

It is a new thing, to be married this way.

New, having participation done with cars l
ike in a drive in movie theater

Our main participants were in one car projected
onto a large screen.

Scott had a twenty five year old blue van with splotched paint and brown primer making a distinct design of no character. His van had an interior smell so bad, you could not even sit in it. Somehow he had gotten used to the terrible odor of dog urine. He was a single person and the sole occupant of the van.

He supplied one witness and showed the ring outside his window allowing Mark to pretend to place it on Sue's finger. She used an old cigar wrapper as a pretend ring.

Second witness was Mark's dad who arrived on a riding mower. It was dripping oil, kicking up dust and he had to turn it off so others could hear what was going on. .

If this event had been filmed, it would have turned tables on science fiction. Dice hanging from Sue and Mark's car swayed above a Saint Christopher magnet on a dashboard.

Mark held tight to skull/crossbones shifting knob and they were announced as "man and wife" as a nephew blew off strings of small firecrackers.

We can never return to normal, it would be too boring.

The Transcendental Property of Being: Day 90

Like a Dream

What you get for practically nothing.
I remembered where. Drove there.
Did not care about parking. Carried my car into store and leaned it out of way in a corner.

Sam, (I gave him a silent name) said hello and that he recognized me.

Of course he had never seen me in his life, before.

He came to life and said: You bet, we have just a perfect stereo sound amplifier for you.

He sent me to another store to pick it up.

At that store, a few blocks away, another Sam met me with so much enthusiasm like he was a brought-back-to-life Lazarus. He led me downstairs and produced an amp covered with centuries of dust that he brushed off with his elbow.

I said that I also needed speakers. He produced two ancient boxes that he said had high and low woofers/tweeters. I shook my head and asked for a microphone. He produced a wrist watch saying: You will need to know exact time when you listen to your new system. I could not figure why? Watch was a Rolex once sold cheap in gas stations. It was cute. I liked it, for only two bucks.

I examined back of amp and quietly thought of my box of red, black and blue cables I had saved, over the years from previous music groups I had bought and abandoned. All connections were familiar to me.

I gave him a hundred dollar bill and he helped me carry all my treasures to where my car was waiting running.

Now, this whole story was precipitated by me wanting to record a song,

which is still running around in my head like a dream.

The Transcendental Property of Being: Day 91

I Am A Writer

Main theme is that I have never hurt anyone
who is disassociated from me.

I did not do harm or bad things to them.

First of all, I do not believe relationships
are meant to last forever.

Secondly, those who cut themselves from me,
did so for their reasons.

Patricia and Lewis were greedy. When they took all I gave them, they did not return one thing to me as appreciation. I have long since recovered from the hundreds of thousands I gave them. I have been given back so much more in money and I hold no grudge against them.

Mary Vonne Sarfatti had much difficulty reconciling my generous nature. She wanted me to not splurge. She tried to get me to save. I do not save. I give my money to people close to me without expecting anything back. I remember a time when I bought dinner for a family sitting at a neighboring table. Mary Vonne got so mad at me that she left and took a cab home. I packed up her meal and drove it to her house immediately. She never thanked me.

Mary would not hold hands as we walked through the woods on nature hikes. She tried to convince me to carry a gun. I did not own a gun. She wanted me to be a hunter. I am not a hunter. I have never hunted.

She and her son were die-hard hunters and she enjoyed killing creatures in the nature center abounding her house.

I used to wonder about how she lived her life. She went back to Germany and had a child by her mother's husband. She did it to try to hurt her mother whom she was jealous of. Whether or not she did this, she raised her son and they became hunters.

I did my best to always remember Mary's birthdays and holidays.

In all the years she was associated with me, I never became intimate with her. Neither of us became attracted to one-another in that manner.

She left off dealing with me because she went, again, back to Germany and married another man who she brought back to Ann Arbor, Michigan and made a home with him.
I wished her well from a distance.

I will tell you that in army life, fellow soldiers always wanted to borrow money. I got tired of lending. So, I put a thousand dollars in a shoe box and told all around me to go into my wall locker and take what they needed, put a slip of paper and when they repaid, take away any slip of paper. In over three years, I never lost one penny out of that thousand dollars.

Michael Thomas

I am sorry for the long winded explanation and I thank you for reading.

I was married for five years then divorced with two children. I married after Vietnam service at a young age. I was confused about life. But, I paid all my child support and saw the children every week. It did no good. My ex-wife still hates me after forty years in between. I still am confused why she hates me other than divorce happens in over fifty percent of all marriages in the world. My divorce was so necessary since I was as unhappy as I could have ever been with her. My marriage was a convenience for my family only, not for me. Even after being divorced, my family still, to this day, blames me for not staying with her.

In my years of running a CPA firm, I had three partners who cheated me. I long ago forgave them and made a financial success for myself without them. All the money they stole from me, was returned by some invisible spirit who watched over me. I am rich to this day despite them.

One of the most redemptive situations, in my life, is my current partner, Staci, who I have worked successively with for over thirty years. She is honest, smart, A CPA and a better partner than any of all who deserted. She is wonderful. I bought her a house for her husband and three children. I made sure she lives in a house with four bedrooms for her three kids. She is comfortable living and comfortable being my partner. She is half my age but twice as smart as me.
I remember Captain Ivy who hated me as a sergeant. I think people that hate me do so because I excel despite their misgivings about me. Ivy once told me: "You would do well if

you reenlist" I said: "It is because of people like you that stops me from staying a soldier"

It is hard to be honest about relationships. Captain Ivy was from West Pointe and he followed rules instead of being aware of dangers that existed in the Jungle surrounding our base camp. I used to tell him that he was going to get himself killed and that I had no intention of following him to the grave. He smirked, I stayed away from him when enemy fire swept over us. I stayed below ground in fox holes.
One of my major accomplishments was publishing books. I was told to stop writing by a close friend. I have never listened to her and I need to write to clear up confusion in my life. I have over twenty books published and I continue to write - as you, who are reading this, can attest to.

The Transcendental Property of Being: Day 92

Uncle John / Aunt Irene

John was my hero,
Irene is, my enemy.
He died long ago.
She hangs on past ninety.

John came back from Patton tanks in 1946.

He took a cab from downtown Detroit at midnight and greeted his wife drunk as he could be.

In the duplex, I was awakened and my six year old heart fell in love with this big burly man who had survived a whole battalion or company that were all killed except for him.
He sat in that room pulling gifts out of his duffel bag and throwing, breaking everything against walls making everybody laugh or cry out loud.

John lived with Irene on one half of our duplex, till he got a job and bought a house three years later. During that time, I could never be torn away from his side. I did everything with him, washing cars, shopping, fixing things.

After he moved I was still his companion and we remodeled inside and outside his new home.

I was young and I would find scrap wood at construction sites and in alleys. I thread pipe and built walls and did electrical work and handed him all the things he needed as we went along.

We poured cement porches and smoothed them out at midnight. We built stairs and put windows in. We converted the attic for his two daughters. I just could not get enough of this man. I loved him and still do long after he died.

One of the elements of John was I placed him above my father because my dad never went into the army. My dad had a deferment because he trained army butchers. Years later I learned to love my father but for a time it was all John.

One of the sad parts of loving John was that his only son died. John never could understand that he had me as a son replacement. And he and his wife never gave me any place of prominence in their family hierarchy. Years went by as I found my own life in marriage and I was never a part of John and Irene's circles.

Thank you for listening to this story.

As I grew, I had articles published in magazines. Irene found them and never congratulated me.

I passed the CPA exam and have over twenty books published. Irene has never recognized my attainments.

For a number of years, I did taxes for Irene and took her to nice dinners,

But, as a CPA I quit doing Irene's taxes when she wanted me to not charge her. Three other members of her family all wanted free work done by me. They were so surprised when I told them all, "No!"

Lastly, for her ninety birthday she invited all her Catholic friends and totally ignored me. I was so insulted that she never even greeted me. Even though I am more Buddhist, I found a lovely religious gift for her, wrapped it nicely and she never thanked me in person or in writing.

You see, very religious people who hold only to one faith, have never examined other beliefs. They hold onto Christ, solely. Buddha, Confucius, Mohammad and so many other faiths from Celtic, Egyptian to Sumerian all have points of view. She did not like how I talked to all her pseudo friends at her party and she quit talking to me and let others tell me she was not my friend.

We keep or lose relationships and I still feel an empty spot in my soul for Irene and John.

In college I learned that Yanomami Indians in South America placed children with aunts and extended family to raise them. They were wise and understanding that parents are sometimes too close to their children to be objective. I often viewed my upbringing with John, similar to this story from Anthropology class.

Things I learned from my father were his patience and persistence. He was an honest man who paid his bills and did his best to raise me. From my father, I learned to center myself.

Things I learned from John, were how to use tools as a builder. That has been invaluable to me over time. John also was an honest man and a hard worker.

My father was a boxer, drinker, brawler, gambler, a man of action. His face was scarred and tough looking. He would take me into the woods or on lakes fishing. He and his friends would catch big fish by trolling. His biggest disappointment was that I never learned to fight or carry a gun. He never understood that I was academic. I watched him carefully and learned to be a good fisherman. My mother made my dad quit gambling and drinking before she would marry him.
I have to inject a funny story here: My father was always rich. During the depression he had money and kept his family fed. My mother's mother came into the grocery store crying because she did not have enough money to bring my mother back from Cuba. My father handed my grandmother six hundred dollars and told her to quit crying and bring her daughter back home. When she did, my dad fell in love with my mother, back from Cuba. And, he married her.

John was a man who knew tools and angles of wood or metal. My father could not tell a flat head from a Philips screw driver. One time a seminal event took place when we had time and I went with John to Lake St Clair spillways with rods, reels, bait and beer. When I spread my blanket and set my rod in place with bobber, I saw that John was having a problem. I rose up, took his rod and set the sinker line, bait and bobber. I cast out for him, put his rod in a holder bracket and went back to my blanket. I had learned how John was human and how he differed from my dad.

It is interesting, but there was a divergent point in my relationship with my mother and father when I had failed in life and for two months I moved back into my parents new home. I spent recovering from my depression and I completely remodeled their home making changes where they both wanted them. I learned that I needed these people who had brought me into a strange world. I now really appreciate and love them. In my case when I grew out of adversity I become vulnerable, turned to family and learned to love.

Again, I truly thank you for reading this writing.

The Transcendental Property of Being: Day 93

We Keep Going and Coming

Words fail - Holy Grail - No trail - Left to avail - Us of meaning

A sunset - Is credit - God's merit - And yet

Life is demeaning - I switch focus - Find new locus –
A red crocus - Fields circus - My eyes beaming

Tomorrow's dreams - Morning dew gleams –
Nature works in teams - Night fades day beams
Life is a bargaining

Let hope be a guide - A soul cannot hide
Eternity's rough ride - Reincarnation is tried
We keep going and coming

Michael Thomas

The Transcendental Property of Being: Day 94

No Echo

Your voice is dead.
Speak but no words come out.
Air surrounding you is as still as a vacuum.
Do not despair, your voice is gone.

It will not come back, no matter how much you cough.
Think about sound. Think since that is all there is to noise.
You speak but no sentences are formed.

You are like a walking ghost who cannot communicate.
There is a grave stone above you inscribed with no epithet.
Say: I am an empty bottle. Like a ship inside a glass cylinder.
Cause is because. A bracelet of invisible bands cinches what once was your throat. Talk into a brick wall. Wave your arms and bellow like a Trojan warrior who has a spear sticking out between his lips.

You are Menelaus leaning over a gunwale of a ship skipping over waves having no fury.

You are Ajax or Achilles and you have expired and been buried in world of fires of ice.

Hear sound of leaves falling upon a ground of decayed vowels. I am going back over instructions to move your eyes and see empty space. Graves in rows mark where your intonations are buried. '

Do not even think of suicide since you will keep coming back mouthless as bitter herbs. Cal to god or Jesus or Buddha and a senseless vagrant will stare at you in frustration. Thief's are hung beside you. Tell them t hat "Amen, I say to you with no parables of wisdom. Let time slide away in sluices of sorrow.

"Your voice is dead. Get used to it. It is permanent. It is here for taking.

There are no rules to this because it is new and final.
Stick your finger into your mouth and vomit,. Nothing will come out since your past is digested into an empty volcano., Curse out bits of vitriol adding up to vapor.

Say that you wish life would come back to you like water from a faucet. It is not connected to meaning. Go back to sleep forever. There is an eternity between your lack of whispering that your cake of meaning has no frosting. Get used to it without crying. Tears fall down a drainpipe of irritation. Collapse into boredom. Come out of a closet of indifference. Destination unknown. Maps with no directions. Engage yourself to a devil who smirks.

Your tablet of commandments gives you free reign to follow no rules. There are no hallways of ancestors hanging in lifelike portraits of motionless resignation.
Your voice is dead over and over until it has no echo.

Michael Thomas

The Transcendental Property of Being: Day 95

What We Cannot See

I do not want to alarm you, but when you left our restaurant we have no intention of making a big issue out of your glancing at any children with their mothers.

We have never had any cases of pedophiles or registered sex offenders being arrested on or near any of our stores. Please let us know if you have any extra secret wishes to kill anyone you came into contact with in any of the booths near you. We have written down your license plate just in case we get called as a witness for any alien abduction incidents by the Department Of Defense agents who monitor extraterrestrial activities.

Pay no attention to Carol who felt your tip was too small. She has a mother who is dying of cancer and just needs a little more money to handle hospital charges. We do not want to make you feel cheap for avoiding the ten percent rule. Our staff feels more secure using methods of determining what to leave as a gratuity. They feel that a total bill should be doubled as a tip. It is a policy in California in areas where famous people do it.

I do want to warn you that walking on train tracks is dangerous. We do not have any railroad near us, but just in case you are walking along fenced areas looking for grape vines to pick leaves for rolling rice dishes cooked, let your ears warn you if you hear engine whistles where there are no swing arms to stop traffic as it passes.

We hope you have enough air in your tires to get to your next destination. A situation of a police chase with shots fired resulted in one patron being hit with a stray bullet piercing his right arm and needing surgery. Luckily he was left handed and continued with his night school exam papers. The bullet passed through and left a dent in his glove box which was covered by a clause in his insurance policy.

You certainly are a very professional person and a stand-out of all our clients. I would dare say that a judge would look with favor upon your reputation as a juror in civil action cases. Your self-efficacious humble demeanor is an indication of a personality free of ego related issues.

Any referrals you make would be looked upon with gratitude. We can only wish for more trouble-free customers to do business with. Please use your name to others you may send our way. We will see if they pan out to becoming long term clients over time.

There is nothing you have overlooked, from where we stand.. We cannot thank you enough for how you handle yourself. From where we judge you cannot be a better person and one we would thoroughly enjoy being paired with on a desert island where there is no need to file tax returns or worry about going to church on major holidays.

Please feel free to include us in your rising or retiring prayers. No need to mention denominations since we all believe in one holy creator of heaven and earth.

You would be welcome at any of our family gatherings. If you come, a name tag will be supplied and we will introduce you to any of our elders.

Let me say, at this time, that no effusive emotion is too little to be inappropriate at any event within scopes of our encounters. Let a rule be followed that we are all in this together and we will overcome adversity to any informal threat of our mutual serenity.

Hallowed be the name of our lord and blessed be his grace over us.

We thank you for coughing into your sleeve and not leaving virus germs on our door knobs or pull handles.

We look forward to having you return to our friendly establishment where we do not judge what we cannot see.

The Transcendental Property of Being: Day 96

Unsatisfied

A young girl naked gets so very boring.
It is exciting to see firm breasts and smooth legs.
Before sickness or age deteriorates.
As they look into a camera dauntless.

They hold long battery looking implements with a speaker microphone end.

They vibrate them over their universal vaginas where we all are born from.

It is a mockery of birthing with all the elements being used for two purposes. We often wonder what in the hell god had in mind giving us falsity just to further a human race.

I remember my father just before he was dead saying to me about the nurse that she had nice boobs,
A friend once told me that two women fingering each other was a most watched scene on our internet.

He also complained that because his wife worked so far away, he had not had sex with her in such a long time, and he truly missed it.

I remember back in 1967 my friend was getting divorced. His wife was just so beautiful. She and I found reason to be in a car alone and resisting my feelings for her was very hard to do. She wanted to fuck me to get even with her husband and I would not let her put me in the middle. I eventually was going to get a divorce. Her name was Carole and I do not regret but I think back on things wondering what would have happened one-way-or-another. She and her companion went on to remarry and have further children and further divorces. I do not believe my friend ever realized how hard it was on me to reject his wife. I was fortunate to be able to recognize the situation for what it was worth, instead of reeling off into a bad situation.

It is so similar in each situation. There is no variation and they all have the same unfinished orgasms that never lead to fulfillment.

We can never get enough of porn yet we get disgusted and turn it off and go to sleep being as unsatisfied as they are.

The Transcendental Property of Being: Day 97

Get The Hell Out Of My Office

In 1962 Forbach gave me a ticket for running through a stop sign.

Fort Greely Alaska, a cold weather testing site, had only one cross street and a whole bunch of broken trails running through the woods for driving test tanks around.

Captain Able shifted in his chair holding the ticket and faced me and Forbach with a queried look on his face.
What does this ticket mean?

Forbach coughed and said the fine was fifteen dollars and a demerit on my 201 file, but no jail time.

There was no holding cell or hoosegow on the compound. Closest jail was in Anchorage, three hundred miles away. Captain Able signaled me to defend myself.

Me: There was no stop sign.

Forbach: It was just covered in snow.

Me: Twenty five feet of snow, to be exact.

Forbach: You knew the sign was under the snow.

Michael Thomas

Me: Sir, there are only three vehicles on the compound: Your jeep, the MP jeep and the company Ford Econoline Van, which I was driving that belongs to the Army.

Forbach: So what?

Me: Well I was going into Fairbanks to get supplies to keep you fed.

Forbach: So what?

Me: Sir, if you let this ticket stand, Forbach will have no one to play cribbage with at night.

Forbach: I will play by myself.

Captain Able: I have had enough of this. Do either of you have anything more to say?

Forbach and me: No

Able ripped up the ticket
and told us to get the hell out of his office.

The Transcendental Property of Being: Day 98

Buddha

Buddha: Every morning we are born again. What we do today is what matters most.

Rabbi: I woke up in jail. Drank coffee in a cafeteria lined with men in chains. I will be born again when my lawyer can get me out of here.

Buddha: No one saves us but ourselves. No one can and no one may. We ourselves must walk the path.

Rabbi: Stones line a path between broken glass alleys. Even garbage trucks will not go down this cement jungle street. I remember playing basketball on a half broken net wobbling on a roof waiting to fall off. We were innocent of youthful fantasies and swore as each shot missed.

Buddha: Hatred does not cease by hatred, but only by love; this is the eternal rule.

Rabbi: Beannie Boys fought with Ravens. These gang fights never made news headlines. They were only noticed by old Mrs Preibie known as "Cat Lady" She would shout from her porch and we would throw empty rusted cans into her back yard and run before she chased us with a broom. At night cats meowed from every corner of her seemingly haunted house.

Michael Thomas

Buddha: Remembering a wrong is like carrying a burden on the mind.

Rabbi: Gordon, a kid from down where we hardly ever went further in our alley. Gordon charged us fifty cents to show us sex behind his garage.   Almost immediately, we all wanted our money back since we all had the same penis.

Buddha: You will not be punished for your anger, you will be punished by your anger.

Rabbi: Bob Sexton stole and held my wallet out to taunt me. I kept reaching for it, till he threw it down quickly. Just as I bent to pick it up, Bob's fist missed my face and we all were awestruck by my surprised look at him as I walked away without a word.

Buddha often says things that get lost in our translation.

The Transcendental Property of Being: Day 99

Pseudonym

Aglaea, Euphrosyne, and Thalia three graces.

Grace, Charm, Beauty

These Greek mythological representations get mixed up in antiquity.

We are three:
        1) who we think we are
        2) who others think we are
        3) who god knows us as

There are three levels of spirituality:

One is that we are aware of all our lives
as reincarnated over and over

Two, that we are aware of only our current life
Three that we drift or float without
any analysis of our deeper self

One thing is certain:
We try so hard to know where we stand in time.

We divide ourselves into being kind to our neighbors and kind
to a god who seemingly made us.

When we examine ourselves and our actions we learn that
there is no difference between life and death. Both sides of
this line are the same: meaning that what exists in one side,
exactly exists on the other side.

Learning that there is no difference between death and life is
a major lesson.

Words lose their meaning
as we internalize all we know inside our consciousness.

This is the last of my poems.

From here I will go on but change what I write
to prose or fiction.

My next writings will be under my alter-ego pseudonym:
Rabbi Schlotz.

The Transcendental Property of Being: Day 100

Nature's Silver Cord

My promise to posterity
Never write about a tree
In whose breast armistice
Fly flags of remembrance
Nor talk about world wars
From sea to shining shores

I will write about spiritualism
Buddha taught existentialism
Marx leads us down a street
Where Employees compete
Oh! Freud? He got jinxed
By Oedipus and Jung nixed

Well not much else to say
Let Odysseus find his way
To Penelope weaving lest
She's forced to marry least
And Agamemnon relented
Coy Helen winked repented

Michael Thomas

Jews and fifty million more
In and out of death's door
Stalin played Gulag's card
And killed many wayward
It seems we are unsatisfied
With all we tortured who died

I am not a major general
Calling Hitler abnormal
He furthered militarism
Our Industrial revolution
We inherited nuclear war
Computers give us more

There's a place where words
Fail to describe our innards
Where poetry is set aside
Revealing intuition inside
And civilizations overlap
Water runs out of our tap

Our toilets no longer flush
We've no more teeth to brush
Silence where once birds
Do not wake or are heard
Evening doves hawks screech
Oceans stop at forest's reach

Do not be swayed or misled
By what you hear or have read
Time is measured by our lies
Condolences for all our cries
Birth to death we drift or float
Religions don't steer our boat

Our marriages end in divorce
Circe sleeps alone of course
She writes letters never sent
And hopes storms will relent
Dido went crazy slit her wrists
As Aeneas sailed to the west

We are sad and all alone
No internet and no phone
Solar storms burnt satellites
Emptiness fills our long nights
Our only hope is to be reborn
Nature's silver cord not torn

Michael Thomas

Author's Biography

Michael G. Thomas is a CPA residing and working in Sterling Heights, Michigan who is best described as a warm and cuddly curmudgeon. He has been writing for decades, primarily poetry and short stories, but has a love of plays and theatre.

Mostly, he defies description, not because he is nondescript, but because the proper words have not been invented. Those who know him well will tell you he is well worth knowing, and that is the best biography one can have.

Website: www.mithomascpa.com

Also by Michael Thomas

ISBN: 978-1500192037

Rabbi Schlotz Talks With God

Michael Thomas

ISBN: 978-1943974726

ISBN: 978-1943974153

Rabbi Schlotz

Talks With Satan

Michael G. Thomas

ISBN: 978-1943974221

ISBN: 978-1943974320

Rabbi Schlotz
Mysteries of Life
Michael Thomas

ISBN: 978-1943974467

ISBN: 978-1492297567

ISBN: 978-1500267889

ISBN-13: 978-1530832071

ISBN: 978-1492776932

ISBN: 978-1495419010

ISBN-13: 978-1501063275

Michael Thomas Poetry
Volume 4

ISBN: 978-1507634387

ISBN: 978-1514174104

ISBN-13:978-1523266333

Michael Thomas Poetry
Volume 7

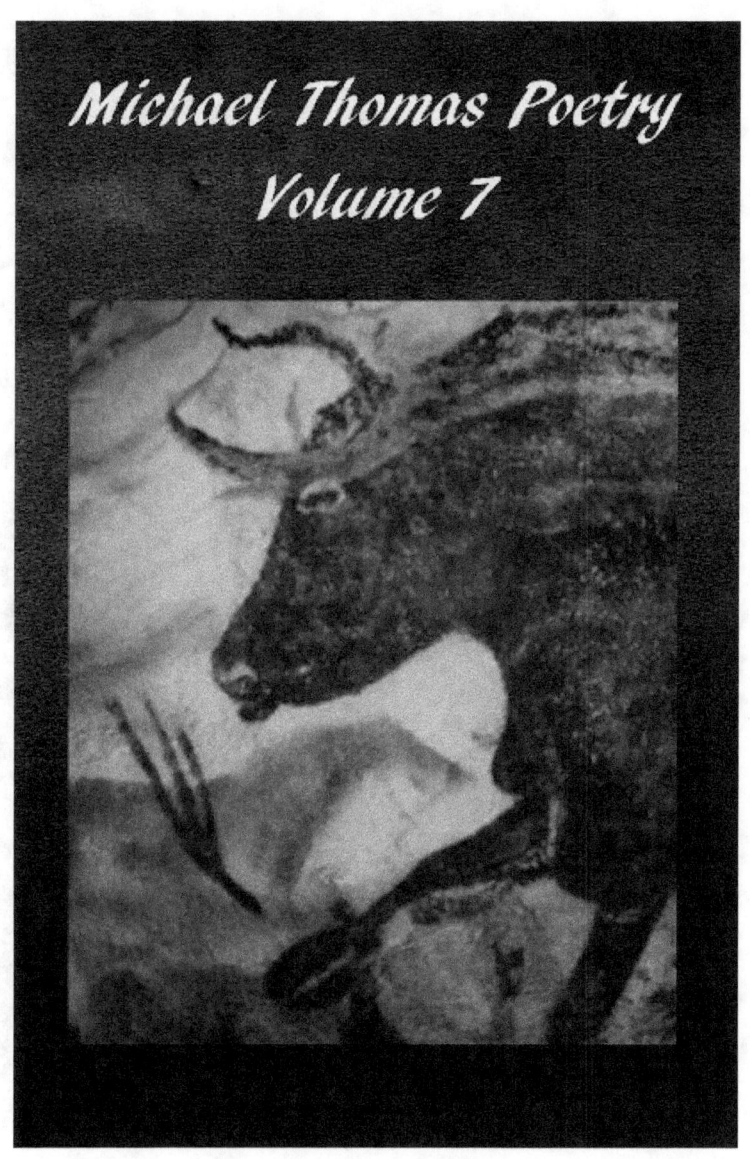

ISBN-13: 978-1-943974-13-9

ISBN: 978-1943974252

Michael Thomas Poetry
Volume 9

ISBN: 978-1943974160

ISBN: 978-1943974337

These and other books by independent authors
can be found at:
www.shoestringbookpublishing.com

Shoestring Book Publishing offers
simple and affordable quality book publishing.

The <u>smart</u> choice
for the <u>wise</u> independent authors voice!

Send your inquiry today to:
Shoestringpublishing4u@gmail.com
Contact Allan 207-922-8837

Please Review!

All independent authors depend upon reviews left on Amazon.com by readers to help promote their books. Without these reviews, they will hardly get any notice. Please take the time to leave a short review. Simply go to Amazon.com, find the book and go to the book's page. Under the author's name will be a list of reviews and stars. Click here and there will be a big button saying "Create your own review". Please click here and review. It only takes a minute!